At Issue

Reproductive
Technologies

D1114264

Other Books in the At Issue Series:

Are Teen Curfews Effective?

Assimilation

Beauty Pageants

Embryonic and Adult Stem Cells

Ethanol

Foster Care

Gay and Lesbian Families

Homeland Security

How Far Should Science Extend the Human Lifespan?

How Should Obesity Be Treated?

How Should the U.S. Proceed in Afghanistan?

Is Parenthood a Right or a Privilege?

Is Selling Body Parts Ethical?

Marijuana

Mental Illness and Criminal Behavior

Nuclear Weapons

The Rising Cost of College

Should the Government Fund Embryonic Stem
Cell Research?

Slavery Today

Teen Suicide

Violent Children

What Role Should the U.S. Play in the Middle East?

At Issue

Reproductive Technologies

Louise I. Gerdes, Book Editor

GREENHAVEN PRESS
A part of Gale, Cengage Learning

Detroit • New York • San Francisco • New Haven, Conn • Waterville, Maine • London

Christine Nasso, *Publisher*
Elizabeth Des Chenes, *Managing Editor*

© 2010 Greenhaven Press, a part of Gale, Cengage Learning.

Gale and Greenhaven Press are registered trademarks used herein under license.

For more information, contact:
Greenhaven Press
27500 Drake Rd.
Farmington Hills, MI 48331-3535
Or you can visit our Internet site at gale.cengage.com

For product information and technology assistance, contact us at

Gale Customer Support, 1-800-877-4253
For permission to use material from this text or product, submit all requests online at
www.cengage.com/permissions

Further permissions questions can be emailed to permissionrequest@cengage.com

Articles in Greenhaven Press anthologies are often edited for length to meet page requirements. In addition, original titles of these works are changed to clearly present the main thesis and to explicitly indicate the author's opinion. Every effort is made to ensure that Greenhaven Press accurately reflects the original intent of the authors. Every effort has been made to trace the owners of copyrighted material.

Cover image © Images.com/Corbis.

LIBRARY OF CONGRESS CATALOGING-IN-PUBLICATION DATA

Reproductive technologies / Louise I. Gerdes, book editor.
    p. cm. -- (At issue)
    Includes bibliographical references and index.
    ISBN 978-0-7377-4436-1 (hardcover)
    ISBN 978-0-7377-4437-8 (pbk.)
    1. Reproductive technology. I. Gerdes, Louise I., 1953-
    RG133.5.R467 2009
    362.198'17806--dc22

                                        2009026341

Printed in the United States of America
1 2 3 4 5 6 7 13 12 11 10 09

Contents

Introduction   7

1. Society Is Embracing   12
   Reproductive Technology
   Gregory Pence

2. Reproductive Technology Is Disturbing   16
   Francis Kane

3. Reproductive Technologies Should   24
   Be Regulated
   Franco Furger and Francis Fukuyama

4. Reproductive Technologies Should Not   33
   Be Regulated
   Ronald Bailey

5. Reproductive Technologies Pose a Threat   39
   to Children's Identities
   Elizabeth Marquardt

6. Reproductive Technologies Do Not Pose   47
   a Threat to Children's Identities
   Josephine Johnston

7. Genetically Designing Babies Is Ethical   55
   Under Certain Circumstances
   Patrick Tucker

8. Genetically Designing Babies   60
   Is Unethical
   Michael Sandel

9. Gender Selection Is Ethical   69
   Norbert Gleicher and David H. Barad

10. Gender Selection Can in Some Cases   76
    Be Unethical
    Preeti Shekar

11. Disposing of Unused Frozen Embryos   81
    Poses Ethical Challenges
    Liza Mundy

12. Freezing Eggs to Delay Motherhood   92
    Should Be Discouraged
    Laura Vanderkam

13. Egg Donation Puts Donors at Risk   96
    Jennifer Schneider

14. Seeking Egg Donors in Developing Nations   105
    Exploits Poor Women
    Antony Barnett and Helena Smith

Organizations to Contact   113
Bibliography   120
Index   126

Introduction

When, in 1997, the first set of septuplets to survive in the United States were born to Bobbi and Kenny Mc-Caughey, the couple received a tremendous outpouring of public support and even gifts—a twelve-passenger minivan, a custom home, and a lifetime supply of diapers. A little over ten years later, in January 2009, Nadya Suleman gave birth to octuplets. The initial celebration of the medical miracle of their birth was short lived. News that Suleman was single, already had six children, and was living with her mother, who had filed for bankruptcy in 2008, led to ridicule of Suleman in the media, where she was dubbed the "Octomom." While many empathized with the frustration of the infertile McCaugheys, political writer Nancy Gibbs observes, many were angry with Suleman because they felt that she "should have been content with her first one or two or three miracle babies rather than going on to mass-manufacture them."

The McCaughey septuplets and the Suleman octuplets were both the result of reproductive technologies. The Mc-Caugheys used fertility drugs. Suleman used in vitro fertilization (IVF), in which eggs and sperm are combined in the laboratory, creating embryos that are then transferred into the uterus. Despite the dramatically different public reactions to these multiple births, both stoked the controversy over the use of these reproductive technologies. The arguments of both defenders and detractors are reflective of other controversies in the reproductive technology debate.

The most common argument against using reproductive technologies that sometimes lead to multiple pregnancies is that these procedures can put both mother and babies at risk. When conducted irresponsibly, bioethicist Scott B. Rae reasons, the use of these reproductive technologies "puts the woman at risk for something that she was not designed for—

carrying 'litters' of children. . . . Furthermore, it puts the babies at risk for something they were not designed for—being born seriously prematurely." Women carrying multiple fetuses run the risk of anemia, blood clots, hypertension, and labor complications. Babies born in multiple deliveries are more likely to develop severe disabilities such as chronic lung disease or cerebral palsy. According to medical commentator Dr. Nancy Snyderman, multiple babies are susceptible to "seizures, jaundice, heart problems, lung problems, blindness, developmental delays—there's a laundry list of things." Some observers also fear the psychological problems these children will face. Some question, for example, whether as a single mother, Suleman can give her children the emotional support that they will need, especially if the eight octuplets face developmental problems and delays. "Undoubtedly these eight children are going to have issues: at the minimum, the issue of neglect," asserts psychiatrist Dr. Gail Saltz.

While fertility experts chastised Michael Kamrava, the doctor who implanted Suleman's embryos, most support what they consider the responsible use of reproductive technologies. Cases such as the Suleman octuplets are rare, they maintain, often performed by outliers. "I would certainly say that [the implantation of eight embryos] is contrary to what everyone else would do in our field," claims fertility-center director Lawrence Werlin. "It was a grave error," said Eleanor Nicoll, a spokesperson for the American Society for Reproductive Medicine (ASRM). "It should not have happened. Eight children should not have been conceived and born." ASRM guidelines for IVF call for no more than two transferred embryos. Indeed, ASRM considers as one of its successes the fact that the number of triplet births declined from 7 percent in 1996 to 2 percent in 2006.

Despite the success of industry guidelines, however, some fertility doctors fear that the public reaction to the octuplets will lead to unnecessary regulation. They contend that fertility doctors already are subject to greater regulation than most physicians. "We're already highly scrutinized," claims fertility-center director David L. Rosenfeld. In fact, he claims, reproductive-medicine specialists are "the only physicians in the country whose numbers are published nationally." In addition, advocates of self-regulation argue, government oversight would restrict advances. "We are probably leaders in the field of reproductive medicine because we can advance without government interference," reasons fertility-center director Angeline Beltsos. "Creating guidelines is critical," she maintains, "but legislating is dangerous."

Some ethicists claim, however, that industry guidelines are not enough. David C. Magnus, director of the Stanford Center for Biomedical Ethics, asserts that the infertility field is poorly regulated. "This is a huge problem," he maintains. Reproductive technology is, in fact, a booming industry in the United States that some claim is worth as much as 3 billion dollars annually. Because the fertility industry is subject to little government regulation, fertility clinics are driven primarily by profit. "You've got a virtually unregulated marketplace," Magnus maintains. The U.S. standards in place are written as recommendations rather than setting out strict rules and sanctions. In truth, professional organizations do not want to take a hard line. However, Magnus claims, "if you leave it up to the marketplace, there will be abuses."

Another argument against reproductive technologies that lead to multiple pregnancies is the enormous economic cost. In the eyes of some observers, the public support for the McCaugheys and scorn for Suleman was a matter of timing. The McCaughey septuplets were born at a time of relative economic security in the United States. Suleman, on the other hand, gave birth to the octuplets during a time of great economic stress. Therefore, these analysts assert, people focused on the McCaughey septuplets as a medical miracle. Due to the economic stress of 2009, however, a public dealing with economic insecurities seemed to be more concerned about who would pay for the Suleman babies. The hospital bill for Suleman's octuplets could run from 1.5 to 3 million dollars. The cost for raising the octuplets will be even greater. "Forget about getting to college; just to get through special-needs stuff—It's going to have to come from somewhere, either the taxpayers of California or her family or her church or the hospital. But she can't do it alone," reasons Snyderman.

In defense of reproductive technology, some commentators claim that multiple pregnancies would be much less likely if insurance covered expensive IVF treatments. Infertility treatments can cost more than $12,000 per cycle. If such treatments are not covered, cash-strapped couples are more likely to choose multiple-embryo implantations to increase their chances of success. According to ethics professor Ronald M. Green, if insurance covered several single-embryo implantations for those struggling with fertility, patients and doctors would be much less likely to implant more embryos at one time. In fact, in most European countries, IVF treatments are paid through universal health-care systems. Doctors in Sweden, for example, perform single-embryo implantation 70 percent of the time. In the United States, doctors perform single-embryo implantation only 3.3 percent of the time. Those numbers would increase in the United States, some reason, if health insurance paid for fertility treatments.

The media celebration of the McCaughey septuplets in the late 1990s was as intense as the media criticism of Suleman following the birth of her octuplets. Both events made public traditionally private concerns. Commenting on the conflicting reactions, political writer Nancy Gibbs questions how easily many were willing to condemn Suleman when these same critics would likely abhor such scrutiny in their own private affairs. Gibbs adroitly remarks, "The decisions we make about parenting are some of the most personal of our lives. These houses are all made of glass, and I'm not sure how many of us

could withstand this level of incoming fire." Nevertheless, defenders and detractors alike have expressed strong views on
both multiple births and the reproductive technologies that
lead to them. The authors in *At Issue: Reproductive Technologies* join this debate, exploring their views on the nature and
scope of reproductive technologies and the policies that will
best inform their use.

1

Society Is Embracing Reproductive Technology

Gregory Pence

Gregory Pence, who teaches bioethics at the University of Alabama School of Medicine in Birmingham, is author of numerous books, including Who's Afraid of Human Cloning?, Flesh of My Flesh: The Ethics of Cloning Humans, *and* How to Build a Better Human: An Ethical Blueprint.

Despite the alarmism that inevitably accompanies new technologies, reproductive medicine continues to be one of the fastest-growing areas of American medicine. In fact, in the face of dire predictions by recognized bioethicists, hundreds of thousands of couples have embraced in vitro fertilization technology. To the frustration of opponents, efforts to rein in reproductive technologies have instead spurred further innovation. By banning federal funding of research using human embryos, for example, private clinics are conducting research without oversight, which in turn has led to more advanced technologies. People should embrace, not fear, reproductive technology and leave regulation to the free market.

Thirty years ago Friday [in July 1978], Louise Brown came into the world amid alarmist predictions that her birth would end sex. Jeremiahs [pessimistic people who foresee a calamitous future] such as writer Jeremy Rifkin wailed that in-vitro ("under glass") fertilization would harm the future Louise. Bioethicist Leon Kass then warned that in-vitro fertilization (IVF), by sundering the bonds between the act of sex and conception, would damage families.

Helping Nature Along

Because of such fears, when Louise's parents walked down the streets of their English town in 1978, their neighbors fled, expecting something scaly or monstrous to be in the baby carriage. When they saw a normal baby, their fears disappeared. "IVF is just helping nature along a bit," Louise's father told them, correctly.

Since then, assisted reproduction has helped along hundreds of thousands of American babies. According to 2005 data from the Centers for Disease Control and Prevention [CDC], assisted reproduction helped create more than 50,000 American babies that year alone.

The Vatican perversely persists in condemning IVF, but it is hard to see the wisdom—or any sense of compassion—behind that thinking. Perhaps no children in history have been so wanted.

Of course, things aren't perfect. Children conceived through IVF have a slightly elevated rate of rare birth defects. It is still not clear why; it could be because of the older age of the eggs and sperm of the parents. But 99% of IVF kids, just like Louise Brown, are born healthy.

Although infertility clinics advertise great rates of success, real figures often disappoint. Few states require insurance companies to cover IVF, and the costs run about $8,000 or more for each attempt. Most couples try two or three times but end in failure. In fact, CDC statistics show that only about 25% to 30% of couples using IVF take home a baby, and if the woman is older than 35, the likelihood is worse.

So physicians have looked for new approaches. The next best tool is using eggs of young women. Such eggs, fertilized by sperm from the older man, create an embryo that can be gestated by the older woman and has a genetic connection to the father. For women over 40, this procedure dramatically increases their chances.

Examining the Alarmism

New medical—especially fertility—techniques are often reported in sky-is-falling prose. In 1969, Warren Kornberg, editor of *Science News*, wrote that ethical questions about assisted reproduction, cloning and human genetics outweighed ethical questions raised by atomic bombs. Whether it is with sperm donations from geniuses, egg donation, babies from thawed eggs, babies from frozen embryos or a baby from a medically twinned embryo, alarmists always predict that the next new technique will take us down the dreaded slippery slope.

The experience of 30 years teaches us [to] discount alarmism about assisted reproduction and embrace . . . new ways of making babies.

Looking back, the alarmism cloaked the real issues, which concerned money. The first involved deception, fraud and greed. Throughout the 1980s, Dr. Cecil Jacobson of Fairfax, Va., used his own sperm instead of the intended fathers' to create as many as 75 embryos. He went to jail for it in 1992. In the mid-'90s, Dr. Ricardo Asch at UC [University of California] Irvine was caught switching donor eggs without women's consent. Asch fled the country to avoid prosecution. The U.S. legal system expunged these fraudulent physicians; further laws wouldn't protect consumers.

There is another issue about money here. Deeply affecting research in assisted reproduction, Congress in 1974 banned the use of federal money in research involving human embryos, a ban that continues.

For such research to occur, then, it had to be done in private clinics that accepted no federal grants but instead got all of their money from client fees. Early on, critics doubted that couples would pay for IVF, especially if their chances of creating a baby were low. The last three decades proved the critics very wrong.

A primal human desire may exist to create a child of one's own. In 1978, most insurance companies resisted paying for IVF as too expensive or frivolous, and critics thought that would halt the practice altogether.

Fortunately, couples enjoy the freedom to spend their money as they choose to buy reproductive help. So, in trying to conceive a child with IVF, some couples drove 15-year-old cars, rented apartments rather than bought houses or went without vacations.

Wholly unintentionally, the U.S. ban on federal funding jump-started innovation in assisted reproduction. One byproduct of the ban was that the National Institutes of Health and ethics committees had no mechanism for regulating research in these private clinics. In Europe, assisted reproduction has always been subject to strict government oversight, and as a result, few innovations occur there. Those in the U.S. opposed to assisted reproduction miscalculated—and wound up creating one of the fastest-growing areas of American medicine fueled, in part, by competing private clinics.

The experience of 30 years teaches us two things: first, discount alarmism about assisted reproduction and embrace (don't fear) new ways of making babies. Second, let the market, not government, regulate baby making. One final note. [In 2007], Louise Brown had her own baby, without assisted reproduction, proving yet again how natural she is.

2

Reproductive Technology Is Disturbing

Francis Kane

Francis Kane is a professor of philosophy at Salisbury University in Maryland and codirector of the university's Institute of Public Affairs and Civic Engagement, which studies the meaning of citizenship and the philosophy and ethics of civic engagement.

Reproductive technology represents a dangerous shift in what it means to be human. In fact, the use of technology blurs the line between human reproduction and the production of commercial products. Creating a child was once a process over which parents had little control. While children conceived in the traditional way share characteristics with their parents, they are also unique. Rather than accept the uniqueness of these children, reproductive technologies allow parents to create the children that they want. Creating children to meet the desires of parents thus poses a threat to human individuality.

In the region where I live and teach on the Eastern Shore of Maryland, the economy centers on a thriving poultry industry. On a number of occasions, when my boys were young, I would trot off with them on a school field trip to admire the wonders of the modern chicken industry. Those experiences in hatcheries and chicken houses came back to me as I was trying to sort through the meaning of some of the newfangled ways humans have devised for their own reproduction—everything from sperm banks to cloning.

Francis Kane, "Begotten, Not Made: The Dangers of Reproductive Technology," *Commonweal*, vol. 135, February 15, 2008, p. 16. Copyright © 2008 Commonweal Publishing Co., Inc. Reproduced by permission of Commonweal Foundation.

As a bioethics teacher, I was familiar with these techniques but felt uneasy and dissatisfied when talking about issues like consent and confidentiality, benefits and costs, ownership and adoption. For what is at stake in the discussion is a great deal more than who owns a frozen embryo when couples divorce, or who will take responsibility for mistakes in human cloning. Far more troubling is the way these new technologies are altering the landscape of human begetting and human self-understanding.

Human cloning will occasion a dramatic transformation of ends and means, for cloning will make the child a means to someone else's end.

Controlling Production

To help get at this unease, more metaphysical than ethical, let's go back to those field trips. What is clear from a cursory look at the poultry industry is that the whole operation is focused on one goal: producing a standardized chicken for the plates of the American consumer. We expect that the Perdue or Holly Farms chicken we buy will be just like the last one and the one before that. To accomplish that goal, the chicken industry (not unlike the automobile industry) has broken down each of the component parts of breeding, hatching, and rendering in an effort to control every variable. All this so that a standard bird arrives on every grocery shelf. Individuality in a chicken is of no value; uniformity is what matters. Thus as little as possible is left to chance, and every part of the production process is controlled and monitored by specialists.

It is not my intent to probe the efficacy of such practices, but I do want to point out that there is arguably a seamless technological line that extends from the production of things like automobiles and chickens to the production of human beings themselves. . . .

A Paradigm Shift

For purposes of contrast, let us look at the two dominant paradigms of birth. In the old-fashioned way (at its best), children were conceived, carried in the womb, and born under the sheltering intimacy of marital love. In the newfangled way, technicians (at their best) break down the old process into its component parts: sperm and egg production; fertilization; implantation; fetal development. In doing so, the whole reproductive process falls under the harsh light of the laboratory. Note the reliance, even fascination, with technical jargon—ART [assisted reproductive technology], IVF (in vitro fertilization), AID (artificial insemination–donor sperm), ICSI (intracytoplasmic sperm injection). One need not believe that the old-fashioned way of having children is the only ethically acceptable one to understand that a real paradigm shift is taking place.

To demonstrate further this technological shift, we can begin with the most extreme example of reproductive technology, cloning, and then work our way back through the seemingly less obnoxious examples. Some years ago, an article in *Time* magazine (February 19, 2001) offered this prophetic thought about the birth of the first human clone:

> At that moment, at least two things will happen—one public, one private. The meaning of what it is to be human—which until now has involved, at the very least, the mysterious melding of two different people's DNA—will shift forever, along with our understanding of the relationship between parents and children, means and ends, ends and beginnings.

The shift that *Time* noted had actually been rumbling underground for years. Still, human cloning will occasion a dramatic transformation of ends and means, for cloning will make the child a means to someone else's end.

In the same article, a Minneapolis marketing specialist spoke of his desire for a clone: "It would be the perfect child to have because I know exactly what I'm getting." If that sounds eerily like a supermarket shopper in the poultry section, that's because the same logic is being applied. The shopper for a clone wants a familiar product, in this case a replica of himself. (The fact that I will never get exactly the "mini-me" I want hardly matters; the result may be imperfect, but the goal is clearly to produce the perfect clone.) A natural event, which guaranteed that our offspring would be unique, irreplaceable, and not totally under our control, is being replaced by a process that insures we get the product we ordered.

When parents wish to replace a dying or dead child, the case for cloning may seem more compelling. But even this is problematic. Either they are successful, and thus compromise the uniqueness of the first child, or they are unsuccessful because the newly cloned child can never fulfill the expectations for the lost child. In either case, what is insidious is the underlying expectation that we can produce a replacement for what has been lost. Unlike replacing a broken toy or an expired goldfish, a cloned replacement strikes at the very heart of our belief in the individuality of each person.

What does it mean that we are now making human beings the way we make thoroughbred race horses?

Seeking Reproductive Control

Human cloning is admittedly an extreme case. Could we not argue that other reproductive strategies are more benign? From the perspective of applied ethics, the answer may be yes; the effects of cloning are far more worrisome than the effects of artificial insemination. When viewed from the paradigmatic shift we have been exploring, however, the example of cloning serves as a *reductio ad absurdum* ["reduction to the absurd," an argumentative technique]. Once we see the overarching goal of reproductive control in the extreme case of cloning, we find it lurking behind other, less alarming forms of ART.

Sex-selection technology is an instructive example. While there may be good therapeutic reasons for avoiding a gender-specific genetic disease like hemophilia, the use of sex selection might more normally be the expression of the desire to have a boy or a girl. (Having had five boys myself, I certainly understand the desire to have a girl!) It seems hardly consequential, this one little effort of control. But is gender a disease? If the child is to be accepted for the gift that she or he is, then might not this "getting what I want" be the first step toward transforming my progeny into my product?

A second example reveals how this trend gathers momentum. You can now go online to peruse egg-donor menus that will help you select the profile of your child's genetic mother. You can select everything from hair color to tanning ability. These Web sites suggest that with the help of technology, you can now design your future child, the way you might design your living room.

Though it hardly raises an eyebrow anymore, even the older technology of sperm donation reveals the underlying moral dilemmas associated with such techniques, which tend to separate procreation from parenting. What does our willingness to create biological orphans really imply? What does it mean that we are now making human beings the way we make thoroughbred race horses? Are we not bothered by the idea of thoroughbred children? Such a technique changes the meaning of human natality, disrupting the whole process of conception, birth, nurturing, and rearing.

Making Ethical Distinctions

My purpose is not to condemn *tout court* [simply] the practices of reproductive technology. There are important ethical distinctions to be made about theme—such as the distinction between technological interventions that eliminate a disease like hemophilia and technological enhancements that produce "designer babies." There is clearly a difference between a technology that supports the natural processes of birth, like artificial insemination with the husband as donor, and those that do not, like sex selection. But the fact that the technology can be put to benign use does not alter the disturbing worldview behind its application. Concern about that worldview can be found on both sides of the conservative-liberal fault line. . . .

How can we think our way out of the technological box we have gotten ourselves into? Not easily. But we can make a start by recognizing the newfangled way of birth for what it is and finding an appropriate response that does not claw away at the authentic meaning of birth and human individuality. . . .

I do not mean to sentimentalize the old-fashioned way of sexual reproduction or to offer a paean to the so-called nuclear family. But the old way did give us moral coordinates. And if the ideal of the nuclear family was seldom achieved in practice, there is little doubt that its goal of engendering and caring for children is still what is called for. There has always been at birth a sense of the child as both "of us" and as "other." The newborn is indeed the fruit of our loins and yet unique. Reproductive technologies tend to upset this delicate balance. In cloning, the "other" is reduced to "me," and in sperm and egg donations, the part of the child that is "of me" is completely alienated from the part that is "other."

Birth is being transformed into a convergent process similar to those we use to produce chickens for the grocery store or cars for the sales room.

Once we act like gods, saying "let us make man in our own image," we begin to reverse the story of Genesis. In Eden, Adam and Eve were instructed not to eat of the tree in the center of the garden. It was the one area of nature not subject to their control. The purveyors of the new birth technologies tempt us to manipulate what we have traditionally let be: the procreative act. They argue they are only facilitating the age-old human desire to have children, that they are only making it easier for certain desired traits to be passed on or introduced in the next generation. After all, choosing a mate also has something to do with the desire to insure certain hoped-for traits in one's progeny.

Clearly, the desire to have a child is one of the most fundamental human drives. But why do we want children, and why should we want them? Because it will keep my boyfriend with me . . . because it will carry on the family name . . . because someday I'll have someone to hitchhike with (a reason actually given by one of my students)—these answers are at best problematic, at worst insidious. They turn the child into a means toward someone else's satisfaction.

Not Beginnings, but Ends

The realm of human motivation is a thicket, and I suspect that often we do not really understand what we are doing when we have a child—until afterward. What is truly frightening, however, is that what was once the superb surprise of birth, the wonder of a new beginning, is now being placed (as Hannah Arendt foretold) squarely under the control of homo faber, "man the maker." Birth is no longer an act of procreation but a production. Rather than a miraculous, open-ended, divergent beginning, birth is being transformed into a convergent process similar to those we use to produce chickens for the grocery store or cars for the sales room. What we have concocted is not a free subject, but a "made" object—one designed according to our whim. To use William May's evocative metaphor, parenting is more dirt farming than engineering. Letting our offspring be who they are is surely a higher calling than learning to make them exactly what we want them to be. That is what the phrase "the miracle of birth" meant: the unprecedented emergence of a unique person whose story would be unpredictable and unrepeatable. As the somewhat hackneyed expression "unconditional love" implies, in having a child we put aside our self-centered goals to welcome a new person who is an end in herself.

In *The City of God*, St. Augustine, reflecting on the book of Genesis, described the awesome power of Creation as the beginning of something wholly new, and he noted that God shared that power with humans: *Initium ut esset, Deus creatus est homo* ("So that there might be a beginning, God created humans"). The miracle is that each birth initiates a new beginning. What our reproductive technologies aim to produce are not true beginnings but predetermined ends. They do not promise unique, unpredictable human beings, only prefabricated images of ourselves as we would like to be. That alone should give us pause.

3

Reproductive Technologies Should Be Regulated

Franco Furger and Francis Fukuyama

Franco Furger is president of Politiken: Technologie-Beratung, a science and technology consulting firm in Lucerne, Switzerland. Francis Fukuyama, an advocate of caution in the use of reproductive technology, is professor of international political economy at Johns Hopkins University. Furger and Fukuyama are the authors of Beyond Bioethics: A Proposal for Modernizing the Regulation of Human Biotechnologies.

Although the scope of reproductive technologies is rapidly expanding, researchers know little about their impact. Because assisted reproductive technologies are clearly evolving from techniques to reduce health risks to customizing and enhancing babies, policy makers should not wait to see if these technologies are harmful. Regulation is necessary to ensure that ethical principles guide the development and use of reproductive technologies. For example, laws should limit the commercial use of eggs, sperm, and embryos; favor biomedical uses over enhancement; and protect the health and well-being of women, children, and embryos. Indeed, governments should ban some technologies, such as human cloning.

In 1995, according to the Centers for Disease Control, over 280 fertility programs operated in the United States. Ten years later, in 2004, this figure had grown to 411, a 47 percent

Franco Furger and Francis Fukuyama, "A Proposal for Modernizing the Regulation of Human Biotechnologies," *The Hastings Center Report*, vol. 37, July 1, 2007, pp. 16–20. Copyright © 2007 Hastings Center. Reproduced by permission.

increase over a ten-year period—although since these figures do not include nonreporting clinics, the actual numbers may be even higher. Should this trend continue, procreation by technological means is likely to become a serious option for a significant fraction of the public.

Doubts About ART

Should we care? Let's begin with a prosaic but important question about the safety of assisted reproductive technologies (ARTs). Practitioners are quick to point out that the safety record of ARTs is excellent. The claim has more than a grain of truth, but on close examination some doubts emerge. Because the industry has never implemented a robust system of health monitoring, it is in no position to reliably assess the health of children born using ARTs. A ... thorough review of the medical literature on this subject, conducted on behalf the American Society for Reproductive Medicine, found essentially no reason for concern, but the study has never been published—only brief summaries of its main findings have been offerered for public scrutiny. As long as "we don't know what we don't know," categorical statements about the safety of ART procedures seem premature.

Still less confidence is possible about the questions raised by the innovative treatments sometimes pressed into service in the quest to satisfy parents' desires. In 2001, for example, news broke that an ART clinic had experimented with ooplasm transfer, a reproductive procedure that relies on the reproductive tissues of three individuals—sperm from a man, nuclear genetic material from a woman, and the cytoplasm (including mitochondrial DNA) of a second, younger woman. Children born through this procedure have three parents, although the fraction of DNA inherited from the third parent is very small.

Other innovations in ART have the effect of expanding the scope of the field from basic assisted reproduction toward customized conception. For example, preimplantation genetic diagnosis [PGD], initially developed to prevent the transmission of dreadful diseases, is increasingly used to prevent minor birth defects and to choose the sex of a baby. ART doctors also rely on PGD to select children for tissue matching—that is, to select children that the parents intend to be tissue donors for older siblings affected by severely debilitating conditions. PGD does not permit literally customized conception, but it certainly gives prospective parents considerably more control over the procreative process.

Meanwhile, some lines of basic medical research could change the biological foundations of human reproduction. . . . A series of experiments has shown that it may be possible to create artificial eggs and sperm from stem cells, which would open up entirely new reproductive possibilities. Lesbian couples could have their own biological descendents, for example. So far, these experiments have been conducted only on animal models, but there is no reason to believe that scientific research will stop there.

Nor should we think that commercialism lags far behind. Already people have spotted lucrative new business opportunities. [In 2006] an entrepreneur in Texas began offering "made-to-order" human embryos. If the present trend continues, the trade in human eggs may become an important source of revenue, at least for low-income women and students. And the sale of sperm can almost be considered a staple of American cultural traditions.

Identifying Appropriate Societal Responses

Libertarians will probably claim that these examples do not justify regulation. In their view, government should intervene only when an activity can be definitively shown to cause harm, and "harm" should be narrowly construed to mean physical harm. To be sure, the excesses of the regulatory state offer many familiar cautionary tales. Nonetheless, the libertarian stance fails to take account of the fact that in reproductive matters, individuals are making decisions not just for themselves, but for others as well. We are all quite accustomed to taking precautions even when we have no definitive proof of an actual harm. We buy earthquake insurance, we exercise regularly, we avoid fatty foods or quit smoking, and we wear helmets while riding bicycles. Governments in all liberal democracies have been operating in a similar way for a long time. In many instances, the risk to an individual may be minimal, but its societal impact may be quite significant.

Conflicts over the use of novel reproductive techniques should be resolved by political institutions, not private entities.

At least in general terms, it is quite clear where reproductive medicine and biomedical research are headed. Over time, more effective reproductive techniques and new cures will become available. Simultaneously, ART technologies will continue to evolve from techniques that merely help people have children to tools for customizing and enhancing their children. We will move toward "reproductive customization," understood literally: couples and increasingly individuals will have at their disposal a range of reproductive techniques to make specific choices about a baby's health and sex, and eventually about other attributes as well, physical or cognitive. As a 2005 report by the Genetics and Public Policy Center demonstrates, the technologies available today to perform human germline genetic modifications (which would be passed through the germ cells from one generation to another) are far from mature. Enhancing higher cognitive traits is certainly beyond our present capabilities, but that will not stop molecular biologists from developing better and faster techniques for modifying the human genome.

Regulatory Responses

Against this background, we believe it would be misguided to take a wait-and-see attitude. It would also be illusory to assume that we can respond by resorting to the arsenal of existing laws and regulations. As we discussed in some detail in our report, *Beyond Bioethics: A Proposal for Modernizing the Regulation of Human Biotechnologies*, the federal statutory system is patchy at best; it was designed only to address concerns about safety and efficacy, not to sort out unfamiliar and difficult ethical dilemmas. State-level laws for their part do not fare much better.

As the history of the regulatory state clearly demonstrates, adopting reactive, sweeping legislation would most likely be counterproductive, as drawing the kind of fine distinctions that many biomedical developments require would become impossible. Nor is self-regulation adequate for this field: conflicts over the use of novel reproductive techniques should be resolved by political institutions, not private entities. For these reasons we believe that a new regulatory architecture is needed. It must be flexible and dynamic yet rooted in broadly acceptable ethical principles, and it must be protected from the political and administrative pitfalls into which regulation on controversial matters easily falls.

What we propose consists of a set of ethical guiding principles, a series of prohibited and regulated activities, and a new regulatory institution. In the enabling legislation, Congress would spell out the ethical principles it considers indispensable to inform the operation of the newly established regulatory agency, identify which activities should be taken off the table up front and which can be performed under suitable regulatory oversight, and establish in some detail the structure of the new regulatory institution. Finally, Congress would also adopt a number of procedures beyond the usual requirements of the Administrative Procedure Act that are designed to ensure agency independency and to prevent administrative drift.

The New Architecture

The ethical principles we have identified in our proposal touch upon several basic aspects of the human experience. They reflect what we believe are widely shared values, not only in the United States but also in many other Western democracies:

- Children's well-being and health should be protected.

- Biomedical procedures on human embryos must respect their intermediate moral status.

- Infertile couples' access to ARTs should be promoted.

- Women's well-being and health should be protected.

- Those making use of ARTs must give free and informed consent.

- Therapeutic uses of biomedicine should be favored over enhancement uses.

- Limits on the commercialization of eggs, sperm, and embryos should be imposed.

Congress should ban up front . . . reproductive cloning, germline genetic modifications, and certain forms of human-animal chimeras and hybrids.

Some of these principles, like protecting the health and well-being of women or requiring informed consent, are hardly controversial. Others, such as ensuring the health and well-being of children, should be considered uncontroversial but are likely to be regarded suspiciously by some. Still more controversial is requiring regulators to favor therapeutic over enhancing applications. We realize that this guiding principle is just that—an obligation to make what in reality may be arduous determinations fraught with ambiguities. But these determinations are no different from the choices that courts are called upon to make in this country on a daily basis. As a matter of practice, even uncontroversial ethical principles such as ensuring the effectiveness of a medical device can raise difficult interpretive questions. Yet the Federal Drug Administration makes such determinations all the time—without having analytical, unambiguous definitions at its disposal.

Finally, we decided to call for regulators to sort out ethical dilemmas based on a view of the embryo as neither a mere clump of cells, nor the moral equivalent of an adult individual. We do not believe an embryo deserves the same legal protection as someone already born. At the same time, it seems to us that an embryo is more than just biological material and deserves a measure of respect. This position—consistent with the view expressed in 1999 by the National Bioethics Advisory Commission in its report on stem cell research–won't satisfy pro-life advocates, but it is defensible and creates a much-needed space for political compromises.

Possible Prohibitions and Regulations

Among the activities we believe Congress should ban up front are reproductive cloning, germline genetic modifications, and certain forms of human-animal chimeras and hybrids. Among the activities to be permitted but regulated is research cloning—that is, somatic cell nuclear transfer for research purposes, preimplantation genetic diagnosis, and biomedical research involving early-stage embryos, among other things. These suggestions are neither exhaustive nor definitive. One could easily imagine prohibiting research cloning, at least for a while, or permitting but strictly regulating certain forms of germline genetic modification, for that matter. Pondering whether elective sex selection should not at least be regulated may also be worthwhile. In our view, which legal and ethical stance Congress might take is ultimately less important than establishing a precedent for making legally binding distinctions between acceptable and unacceptable reproductive practices. . . .

Failure to ensure that all societal perspectives are heard is a problem not limited to reproductive medicine or biomedical research; it is quite common across the regulatory state. Regulatory agencies from the Environmental Protection Agency to the Department of Energy and the Occupation, Safety and Health Administration have a long history of producing regulatory decisions driven by the most influential interest groups, to the detriment of the public at large. Commentators and practitioners have long ignored this phenomenon, however, for two main reasons. With the arrival of the theory of public choice in the 1960s, scholars of the administrative state largely abandoned the thought that regulatory and political action was based on the notion of public interest; they held instead that nothing more than the aggregation of self-interested motives explained what went on in government.

Decisions about reproductive ethics ... concern the future of mankind. They should not be left simply to individuals and the market.

Some find this analysis of politics excessively cynical, but it has been tremendously successful in illuminating many administrative and political phenomena. On the other hand, it has prevented scholars and practitioners alike from focusing on serious shortcomings of our regulatory system, such as capture by special interests. If the concept of public interest is held to be vacuous, then politics is nothing but a war between different special interests, and the only possible way of explaining a political outcome is to identify which interests won out. Our discussion suggests that, conceptual difficulties notwithstanding, it is easy to point to cases in which the public interest is being systematically ignored.

A second important reason for ignoring the failure to look beyond special interests is that there seemed to be no practicable way to correct the problem. Until recently, no viable options were available to mobilize a large, unorganized political constituency. Information technologies are now changing all this. For the first time in the history of modern liberal democracies, it is becoming possible for the public to take on an active role in politics outside regular elections and referenda. This possibility should be taken seriously and put to use. Internet telephony, combined with e-collaboration solutions, makes bringing together a large number of citizens fairly easy.

In this way, we can move decisions about reproductive ethics into the political realm, where they can be debated by the broader community. These decisions concern the future of mankind. They should not be left simply to individuals and the market.

4

Reproductive Technologies Should Not Be Regulated

Ronald Bailey

Ronald Bailey is a science correspondent for Reason, *a magazine that promotes libertarian principles such as a free market and individual freedom.*

Proposals to regulate reproductive technologies without concrete evidence of harm are unnecessary. U.S. laws regulating human reproduction have a shameful history. For example, the U.S. Supreme Court in 1927 upheld forced sterilization. It wasn't until the 1960s that the Court began to overturn laws that restricted personal reproductive decisions. Attempts to regulate these technologies are simply a means to allow those who oppose reproductive technology to impose their moral choices on others and are a step backward for the United States. People should therefore oppose the creation of an agency to monitor personal reproductive choice.

"We are proposing a new regulatory institution in Washington, DC," said Francis Fukuyama, professor of political economy at the Johns Hopkins University School of Advanced International Studies and author of *Our Posthuman Future*. "It's been a long time since anyone has done that."

What needs regulating? Human biotechnology. Fukuyama unveiled his plan for a new agency at a conference held at the

Ronald Bailey, "Medievalizing Biotech Regulation," *ReasonOnline*, March 9, 2007. Copyright © 2007 by Reason Foundation, 3415 S. Sepulveda Blvd., Suite 400, Los Angeles, CA 90034, www.reason.com. Reproduced by permission.

Rayburn House Office Building on Capitol Hill. The blueprint for the new biotech regulatory agency being proposed by Fukuyama and Swiss technology consultant Franco Furger is laid out in a 400-page book, *Beyond Bioethics: A Proposal for Modernizing the Regulation of Human Biotechnologies.*

Why do we need a new biotech regulatory agency? Because bad things have happened? Not at all. In fact, Fukuyama wants to put his proposal in play now so that the denizens of Capitol Hill can simply pull it off the shelf and enact it into law when some sort of biotech scandal erupts. The proposed agency is explicitly modeled after the British Human Fertilisation and Embryology Authority (HFEA). Fukuyama's new agency would not just regulate the safety and efficacy of new biotechnologies, but also rule on their ethical propriety. According to Fukuyama, biotechnology is "galloping ahead" and it's time to move from ethical discussions to regulation and "social control."

Furger discussed some recent developments to illustrate how biotech is galloping ahead. For example, a Texas fertility clinic is now offering embryos for sale; researchers have manufactured mouse sperm from stem cells; and others have inserted human cell nuclei into rabbit eggs to try to produce stem cells. Furger said that he was listing these activities, "not to say that they are reproachable. Some may be acceptable and some not." He asked, "But how do we make that determination?"

Regulating ART

Fukuyama explained that the new agency would regulate anything having to do with assisted reproduction techniques (ART). This would include IVF [in vitro fertilization], ooplasm transfer, sex selection either by pre-implantation genetic diagnosis (PGD) or sperm sorting. The agency would also regulate research involving human reproductive tissues including all embryonic stem cell research and anything dealing with human developmental biology.

"Biotech has reached the point where existing regulators, the Food and Drug Administration and the National Institutes of Health, can't handle it," declared Fukuyama. The agency would be guided by a set of ranked ethical principles. Its first concern would be the well-being and health of children. Second, ensuring equal access to ART for infertile couples. Third, protecting the well-being of and health of women. Fourth, promoting therapeutic uses of ART over enhancement uses. Fifth, making sure that patients and research subjects give their free informed consent to procedures. And finally, advocating for regulations to limit the commercialization of human eggs, sperm and embryos.

Fukuyama would completely ban human reproductive cloning, the creation of human-animal chimeras for the purpose of reproduction, germline genetic modifications, any procedure that would alter the genetic relationship of parents to children, and the patenting of human embryos.

Do we really want a federal agency making and imposing ethical decisions about human reproduction?

The new agency would regulate research cloning, PGD, sex selection of embryos, and the commercialization of certain elements of human reproduction such as the sale of eggs, sperm and embryos. It would consist of a set of commissioners, appointed by the president and advised by a board consisting of various stakeholder groups such as patients, ART practitioners, the scientific community and the biotech industry. Fukuyama also introduced a novel set of mechanisms for consulting with the wider public including deliberative panels and a consultative college consisting of randomly selected members of the public who convene to consider regulatory issues over the internet.

Instead of inhibiting research and the development of new treatments, the new agency could spur them on, suggested

Fukuyama. For example, he asserted that Britain is ahead of the United States in human embryonic stem cell research because of the HFEA's regulations. Fukuyama is just plain wrong about that. The *Guardian* reported [in March 2007 that] "Excessive bureaucracy imposed by the Human Fertilisation and Embryology Authority [is] prohibiting development in stem cell research and threatening Britain's position as a world leader in the field." The *Guardian* quoted stem cell researcher Alison Murdoch, director of the Newcastle Centre for Life fertility clinic, as saying, "The way the government has handled the work we do is to regulate it to the point that it looks like it's got barbed wire around it."

A Wretched History of Regulation

But what about the larger question: Do we really want a federal agency making and imposing ethical decisions about human reproduction? Consider the wretched history of federal and state regulation in this area. In 1873, Congress passed the Comstock Laws that outlawed "every obscene, lewd, or lascivious, and every filthy book, pamphlet, picture, paper, letter, writing, print, or other publication of an indecent character, and every article or thing designed, adapted, or intended for preventing conception or producing abortion." The Comstock Laws authorized the U.S. Post Office to confiscate any publications providing advice on contraception and condoms shipped through the mail. The first eugenics law was passed in Indiana in 1907 and eventually laws allowing the forced sterilization of "unfit" people were adopted by 30 states. Infamously, the U.S. Supreme Court upheld forced sterilization in the case of *Buck v. Bell* in 1927. By the 1960s, some 66,000 Americans had been forcibly neutered.

In the last half of the 20th century, the U.S. Supreme Court finally stepped in to overrule state interference in the reproductive decisions of Americans. In 1965, the Court found unconstitutional the Connecticut law prohibiting use of birth control by married couples in *Griswold v. Connecticut*. In 1967, the Court ruled in *Loving v. Virginia* that the laws in 16 states banning interracial marriage were unconstitutional. In 1972, the Court struck down in the case of *Eisenstadt v. Baird* a Massachusetts law prohibiting the sale of contraceptives to unmarried people. And of course, the Supreme Court found prohibitions on abortion unconstitutional in 1973 in *Roe v. Wade*.

What [advocates for government regulation are] proposing is a step backward to the bad old days in which strangers get to vote on what kind of children their fellow citizens will be allowed to bring into the world.

Imposing Moral Choices

The HFEA, the model for Fukuyama's new biotech regulatory agency, has similarly interfered with the reproductive decisions of British people. The HFEA has told couples that they could not select the sex of embryos to be implanted. Even now the parents wanting to use PGD to insure that their children will not be burdened with an inherited genetic disease must apply for permission from the HFEA. And the HFEA has banned paying women for providing eggs to be used in research.

Fukuyama's agency would rule not only on safety and efficacy but on moral questions surrounding human reproduction. Some possible techniques are objectionable and should be banned, e.g., any attempt to create a half-human half-chimp baby. On the other hand, Fukuyama wants to ban ever allowing parents to safely choose genes that would tend to give their children healthier immune systems, stronger bodies and cleverer brains.

It turns out that the proposed agency is largely just a vehicle for Fukuyama to impose his moral choices on other people. What Fukuyama is proposing is a step backward to the bad old days in which strangers get to vote on what kind of children their fellow citizens will be allowed to bring into the world. A government bureaucracy, rather than parents, would get to make eugenic decisions. As the sorry history of attempts to regulate human reproduction shows, the truly moral thing to do is fiercely resist this proposal.

5

Reproductive Technologies Pose a Threat to Children's Identities

Elizabeth Marquardt

Elizabeth Marquardt is vice president for family studies and director of the Center for Marriage and Families at the Institute for American Values, an organization focused on children, families, and civil society. Marquardt has shared her views on television and radio programs and in the New York Times, *the* Washington Post, *the* Los Angeles Times, *and* Reader's Digest.

Because they alter the meaning of parenthood, reproductive technologies pose a threat to children. Parenthood, once an institution designed for the benefit of children, is now one in which parents claim a right to have children. Without the child's consent, infertile parents use egg and sperm donors, surrogates, and other reproductive technologies that separate children from one or both of their biological parents. Some donor-conceived children claim that these technologies deny them a better understanding of themselves. Indeed, stories told by donor-conceived children suggest that children are better off when they know their biological mother and father.

Why should we be concerned about the many rulings, laws, and proposals around the world that are aimed at redefining parenthood?

Elizabeth Marquardt, *The Revolution in Parenthood: The Emerging Global Clash Between Adult Rights and Children's Needs*, New York, NY: Institute for American Values, 2006. Copyright © 2006, Institute for American Values. All rights reserved. Reproduced by permission.

Defining the Rights of Children

A good society protects the interests of its most vulnerable citizens, especially children. Right now, the institution that is most core to children's very survival—that of parenthood—is being fundamentally redefined with the state giving its implicit support and at times leading the way. In law and culture, parenthood is increasingly understood to be an institution oriented primarily around adults' rights *to* children rather than children's need *for* their mother and father. These extraordinary moves are being made largely absent any real public awareness or debate.

The common thread running through many of these decisions is the adult right to a child. These rights claims are important. The desire for a child is a powerful force felt deep in the soul. The inability to bear a child of one's own is often felt as an enormous loss, one that some grieve for a lifetime. These desires must be responded to with respect and compassion. The claim that medicine and society should help those who cannot bear children is a legitimate one.

But the rights and needs of adults who wish to bear children are not the only part of the story.

Children, too, have rights and needs. For example, the United Nations Convention on the Rights of the Child, ratified in 1989, states that "the child shall . . . have the right from birth to a name, the right to acquire a nationality and, as far as possible, the right to know and be cared for by his or her parents." The authors of the convention understood several key features necessary to human identity, security, and flourishing—having a name, being a citizen of a nation whose laws protect you, and, whenever possible, being raised by the two people whose physical union made you.

Adults who support the use of new technologies to bear children sometimes say that biology does not matter to children, that all children need is a loving family. Yet biology clearly matters to the adults who sometimes go to extreme lengths—undergoing high-risk medical procedures; procuring eggs, sperm, or wombs from strangers; and paying quite a lot of money—to create a child genetically related to at least one of them. In a striking contradiction, these same people will often insist that the child's biological relationship to an absent donor father or mother should not really matter to the child.

Defining Parenthood

Of course, there is a very real and urgent role for the state to play in defining parenthood. Some biological parents present a danger to their children or are otherwise unable to raise them. Adoption is a pro-child social institution that finds parents for children who desperately need them. Adoption is a highly admirable expression of altruistic love, a kind of love that transcends our hardwired tendencies to protect our blood relations above all others. But the existence of legal adoption was never intended to support the argument that children don't care who their fathers and mothers are, or to justify the planned separation of children from biological mothers and fathers before the children are even *conceived.*

Many are now speaking out about the powerful impact on children's identity when adults purposefully conceive a child with the clear intention of separating that child from a biological parent.

Certainly, biology is not everything. It does not and should not determine the full extent or depth of human relationships. Biological parents are tragically capable of harming their children, and some children are better off removed from these parents (though, as we will see, children on average are far safer with their biological parents than with unrelated adults). But the actions and testimony of children and adults often powerfully suggest that biology does matter.

In the current rush to redefine parenthood, we must stop to ask critical, child-centered questions: Are children's understandings of parenthood as flexible as those who pose these issues mainly as a matter of adult rights believe them to be? How do children feel about the brave new world of parenthood? Does how they feel matter?

The Child's Point of View

Children raised without their own married mother and father often have perspectives about their lives that are radically different from how the legal scholars, courts, and would-be parents expected they would feel. For example, studies on the inner lives of children of divorce are showing an enormous downside for children that was never considered in the heady, early days of the no-fault divorce revolution.

To be perfectly clear, the question is *not* whether children love the parents who raise them. Children almost universally and unquestioningly love their parents, whether their parents are married, divorced, single, gay or straight. Rather, the question is how children feel and how they make sense of their identities when their mother or father (or both) is absent from their daily lives.

The first generation of donor-conceived children who are now coming of age form a remarkable case study to explore this question. Most in this first generation were conceived by married heterosexual couples using donor sperm. Anecdotally, many are now speaking out about the powerful impact on children's identity when adults purposefully conceive a child with the clear intention of separating that child from a biological parent. These young people often say they were denied the birthright of being raised by or at least knowing about their biological fathers. They say that this intentional denial profoundly shapes their quest to understand who they are.

Donor-conceived teenagers and adults are forming organizations, are frequently quoted in news articles, and are using the Internet to try to contact their sperm donors and find half-siblings conceived with the same sperm. They hail from the United States, Canada, Australia, Britain, Japan, and elsewhere. Numbers are hard to come by, but estimates are that the number of children now born in the U.S. each year through artificial insemination range from 30,000 to 75,000 and that about 3,000 each year are conceived using donor eggs. While the numbers arguably are small, they are growing, and the stories these young people tell raise questions not only about their own experience but also about the prospects for the next generation of children born of still more complex reproductive technologies.

" . . . the pain of infertility should not be appeased at the expense of the next generation."

Donor-conceived young people point out that the informed consent of the most vulnerable party—the child—is not obtained in reproductive technology procedures that intentionally separate children from one or both of their biological parents. They ask how the state can aid and defend a practice that denies them their birthright to know and be raised by their own parents and that forcibly conceals half of their genetic heritage. Some call themselves "lopsided" or "half adopted." At least one uses the term "kinship slave." Some born of lesbian or gay parents call themselves "queer spawn," although others in the same situation find the term offensive. No studies have been conducted focusing on these young people's long-term emotional experience. Clearly, rigorous long-term studies need to be done. For now, we should listen to their compelling voices.

Telling Their Stories

Narelle Grech, an Australian donor-conceived woman in her early twenties, asks, "How can you create a child with the full knowledge that he or she will not be able to know about their history and themselves?" She wonders what social message the practice of donor conception gives young men: "Will they think it's OK to get a woman or girl pregnant and that it would be OK to walk away from her, because after all, biology doesn't matter?"

A fellow Australian, Joanna Rose, asks why everyone "flips out" when the wrong baby is taken home from the hospital, yet assumes that donor-conceived children are just fine. She argues: "Our need to know and be known by our genetic relatives is as strong and relevant as anyone else's." She writes, movingly, "I believe that the pain of infertility should not be appeased at the expense of the next generation."

In interviews, donor-conceived young adults often say something like this: My sperm donor is "half of who I am." One young woman known as Claire is believed to be the first donor offspring to benefit from open-identity sperm donation and have the ability to contact her father upon turning 18. She says she wants to meet her donor because she wants to know "what half of me is, what half of me comes from." Eighteen-year-old Zannah Merricks of London, England says, "I want to meet the donor because I want to know the other half of where I'm from." Lindsay Greenawalt, a young woman from Canton, Ohio who is seeking information about her sperm donor, says, "I feel my right to know who I am and where I come from has been taken away from me."

"It scares me to think I may have brothers or sisters out there, and that he [my father] may not care that I exist."

Eve Andrews, a 17-year-old in Texas, plans to ask the California sperm bank that aided in her conception to forward a letter to her donor when she turns 18. "There's a lot of unanswered questions in my life and I guess I want the answers," she explains. By contrast, her 51-year-old mother, interviewed for the same story, says, "As a woman dealing with the prospect of infertility, all you want is that baby. . . . It never even occurred to me this child might want to find her biological father someday."

One young man, a 31-year-old doctor in Japan, learned that he was conceived by donor sperm when he examined his parents' white blood cell group while studying medicine. "The most painful thing was the fact that my parents didn't tell me for 29 years," he said. "Unless I was told by my parents, I couldn't even exercise my right to know my biological origin."

A 14-year-old girl in Pennsylvania wrote to Dear Abby after finding out she was conceived with donor sperm. In just a few sentences she identified some of the enormous identity issues that confront donor-conceived young people and that are now a challenge to our society. She wrote: "It scares me to think I may have brothers or sisters out there, and that he [my father] may not care that I exist." This young teenager, struggling alone with feelings of abandonment, grief, and confusion, poignantly challenged the current legal and social position on this issue: "I don't understand why it's legal to just donate when a child may be born."

Some observers respond to the voices of donor-conceived adults by saying that there is an inherent contradiction in their argument. These observers say that donor-conceived persons who question the practice of donor conception are wishing away their own existence, and that without the use of a sperm or egg donor or surrogate these young people would not be alive. I find this response highly insensitive. All of us, no matter how we arrived here, should be able to share our stories and struggles in an atmosphere of respect and dignity without being told that we are irrationally ignoring the process that gave us life or are failing to show sufficient appreciation for our life.

The Importance of Biological Parents

From a social scientific point of view, what do we know about children's experiences when they do not grow up with their own mother and father? In many areas we know a great deal. In some, we need to learn more.

In recent decades a powerful consensus among social scientists has emerged about the benefits of marriage for children. The *New York Times* not long ago reported: "From a child's point of view, according to a growing body of social science research, the most supportive household is one with two biological parents in a low-conflict marriage."

Children raised by divorced or never-married parents face an increased risk of living in poverty, failing in school, suffering psychological distress and mental illness, and getting involved in crime. Children raised outside a married family are less likely to graduate from college and achieve high-status jobs. When they grow up, they are more likely to divorce or become unwed parents.

In terms of children's physical health and well-being, marriage is associated with a sharply lower risk of infant mortality, and children living with their own married parents are more physically healthy, on average, than children in other kinds of families. Most tragically, children not living with their own two married parents are at significantly greater risk of child abuse and suicide. . . .

With regard to children conceived with donor sperm, a donor egg, or a surrogate mother, as yet there are no data on these children's long-term, emotional well-being. Researchers should listen to the stories that are beginning to emerge and undertake rigorous studies of their experiences.

We have more to learn. But evidence and sensitive observations of children's lives strongly suggest the importance to children of recognizing their need to be raised, whenever possible, by their own mother and father.

6

Reproductive Technologies Do Not Pose a Threat to Children's Identities

Josephine Johnston

Josephine Johnston explores legal questions involving bioethical issues at the Hastings Center, a bioethics research institute. The Center examines ethical issues in the areas of health, medicine, and the environment.

Having genetic parents use reproductive technologies need not pose a threat to a child's identity. Banning technologies that create children who are not genetically related to only one man and one woman are therefore unnecessary. Children whose genetic material comes from two men or one man and two women will, of course, be different. However, difference does not mean deviance unless society unfairly creates such a label as it once made outcasts of the children of unmarried mothers or interracial couples. Children of different genetic origins will be loved and in today's egalitarian society need not feel like outcasts.

Although [Francis] Fukuyama and [Franco] Furger are not the first to suggest that the interests of children should be among the most pressing concerns attending assisted reproduction, their decision to stress children's well-being and health is still noteworthy and commendable. In a business motivated strongly by the interests of would-be parents, they do well to remind us that the intended results of assisted re-

Josephine Johnston, "Tied Up in Nots over Genetic Parentage," *The Hastings Center Report*, vol. 37, July 1, 2007, pp. 28–31. Copyright © 2007 Hastings Center. Reproduced by permission.

production are future persons who must live intimately with the decisions of their parents, fertility services providers, and any egg, sperm, embryo, or other donors involved in their creation.

What I find strange about their proposal for regulating reprogenetics, however, is one of the prohibitions that they suggest is key to safeguarding children's interests.

Fukuyama and Furger do not set out very many substantive recommendations as to what should be prohibited, permitted, or regulated. They focus instead on detailing the regulatory mechanism itself. Nevertheless, they identify general ethical principles that the regulatory system should promote and a few targets for prohibition and regulation that follow from these ethical principles. In addition to banning reproductive cloning, the creation of human-animal chimeras [hybrids] for reproductive purposes, germline modification, and the parenting of human embryos, they seek to outlaw the creation of children who are not the genetic offspring of one man and one woman. Anything else—the creation of a child with genetic material from two men, or two women, or one man and two women, and so on—would violate both a "fundamental biological principle" and the moral commitment to protecting the health and well-being of children.

The legal system, the fertility industry, and much of society now recognize the social parents as the legitimate parents and release the donors and surrogates from any parental rights.

The Rights of Genetic and Social Parents

In the early days of assisted reproduction, the use of donor sperm prompted questions about parentage: who is the "father"—the sperm donor or the man who will help raise the child? Indeed, until the law clarified that the man who intends to raise the child is the legal father, some fertility clinics would mix the sperm of a few donors together so that no one could know which donor had fathered the child.

Similar questions were raised by egg and embryo donation and surrogate gestation: who is the "real mother"—the egg donor, the woman who gestates the child, or the woman who intends to raise the child? While not always as easy to solve as parentage questions in the sperm donation context, we have generally come to recognize the intended parents as the legal and social parents of any child born from donated gametes or embryos, and the donors are understood simply as donors, or as "genetic parents" or "biological parents" or—in the case of a gestational surrogate—as the "gestating mother." These terms are still somewhat problematic and contested—in part because we usually give so much responsibility to anybody identified as a parent—but it is fair to say that the legal system, the fertility industry, and much of society now recognize the social parents as the legitimate parents and release the donors and surrogates from any parental rights and responsibilities.

Regulating Novel Genetic Origins

Now, Fukuyama and Furger warn, "There are a number of technologies emerging that will make possible the creation of children who are not the offspring of one man and one woman, as every human child has been up to now in the history of our species." The problem for Fukuyama and Furger is apparently not that these technologies introduce the need for a distinction between biological or genetic parents on the one hand and legal or social parents on the other. The problem is that the child will have been created by combining genetic material from persons other than one man and one woman.

An example of such a technology that is already in use is ooplasm transfer, a technique employed to circumvent problems in some women's eggs that involves replacing the nucleus of a donor's egg with the nucleus of another woman's egg (usually the intended mother's). The egg is then fertilized with sperm (usually from the intended father) and the embryo is transferred for gestation. Any child born will have received genetic material from three people: the man whose sperm fertilized the egg, the woman who was the egg donor, and the woman whose egg's nucleus was used. In the future, it may be possible to create eggs or sperm from stem cells; if that technique were used to create children with two genetic "mothers" or two genetic "fathers," it, too, would breach Fukuyama and Furger's proposed prohibition. Because their concern is the creation of children who do not have just one genetic mother and one genetic father, we have to assume that using this technology to create a child from the stem cells of a heterosexual couple would be permissible. But using it to let a homosexual couple have a child who is genetically related to both parents would be prohibited.

[Opponents do not] give evidence for why it might be so disturbing to know that your genetic parents were two men, or two women, or one man and two women.

Fukuyama and Furger are light on justifications for their proposed prohibition (which is in some ways to be expected, given that they are more interested in the regulatory mechanism than in the substance of the prohibitions). They argue that such a child would not, on the question of genetic origins, be the same "as every human child has been up to now in the history of our species," but they do not explain why it is important to maintain this particular feature of human reproduction. It cannot be a concern to protect natural procreation in general, or they would have to oppose fertility treatment, which actively seeks to circumvent natural (biological) barriers to reproducing. Similarly, an opposition to manufacturing children could apply to all in vitro fertilization, where embryos are created in laboratories rather than inside a woman's body.

They say that they are concerned about the impact of novel genetic origins on children's "psychological development and on the development of their identities," but they do not unpack this concern or give evidence for why it might be so disturbing to know that your genetic parents were two men, or two women, or one man and two women. They certainly do not explain why the nature of a person's genetic origins might be as important as, or more important than, say, the family environment in which she grows up.

The Right to Opposite-Sex Parents

Another scholar who has expressed concern about the impact of fertility treatment on the well-being of children is Sidney Callahan. Like Fukuyama and Furger, Callahan considers the genetic "parentage" of children to be important. But unlike Fukuyama and Furger, Callahan is opposed to all use of sperm, egg, and embryo donors because she believes both that children should be created from the egg of a woman and the sperm of a man and that they should be raised by these very same individuals. Instead of focusing on the origins of the genetic material that was combined to produce a child, Callahan is concerned about the relationship between the child and her parents, which she believes is ideally both genetic and social. She is not opposed to adoption, which she characterizes as "rescuing" a child, but she thinks that we should not set out to sever the link between a child and her genetic parents.

Fukuyama and Furger, on the other hand, make clear that they do *not* wish to ban the intentional creation of families in which one or both of the parents is genetically unrelated to the child. Their goal is to regulate the genetic makeup of children. They believe that "every child has the right to be biologically related to a mother and a father even though they may be brought up in a variety of households in which the biological mother and father may be absent." With this proviso, they allow for the possibility of same-sex parents, just not same-sex genetic parents.

Creating Illegal Beings

The closest thing to Fukuyama and Furger's proposed prohibition is probably the wildly popular opposition to reproductive cloning, which is similarly rooted in a concern about the supposed psychological harm caused by the nature of a person's genetic origins. Opposition is expressed to the fact that a cloned child would be almost identical genetically to an existing, or deceased, person. Such a child, it is argued, would not have an "open future" because someone with the same genes would already have existed, and the cloned child might feel as though his own life is therefore predestined or constrained (commentators tend to assume that the child would know he is a clone).

The question about an open future is presumably not a concern for children with three genetic parents—their future might be even more open than ours—but like a clone, any child who knows that her genetic parents were two men, or one man and two women, would know that in this way she is different from the rest of us. But it is not obvious to me that knowing about this difference need be harmful to the child—unless, of course, we tell her that this difference is deviant.

Unless we tell children that, due to how they were created, they are flawed or incomplete persons, what will really matter is that these children are loved.

In her book *Illegal Beings: Human Clones and the Law*, law professor Kerry Lynn Macintosh argues that the most common objections to cloning are "false or exaggerated," reflecting and inspiring "unjustified stereotypes about human clones" that stigmatize clones as subhuman and injure "the egalitarianism upon which our society is based." She begins by quoting law professor Laurence Tribe, who in a 1998 essay made the argument that one risk of bans on particular methods for making human babies is that such babies will still be born, only to find themselves "potential outcasts—persons whose very *existence* the society has chosen, through its legal system, to label as a misfortune and, in essence, to condemn." Tribe describes the high price paid by children born to unwed women or to interracial couples and asks, "How much higher would that price be when the basis on which the law decides to condemn a given baby-making method (like cloning) is . . . the far more personalized and stigmatizing judgment that *the baby itself*—the child that will result from the condemned method—is morally incomplete or existentially flawed by virtue of its unnaturally manmade and deliberately determined (as opposed to 'open') origin and character?" One might make a very similar argument against the ban proposed by Fukuyama and Furger.

What Really Matters

Many of the techniques that Fukuyama and Furger would like to ban have not been shown to work in humans, and developing them further might well endanger the health of any woman made pregnant through them or any child born with their aid. Until these health risks are resolved, opposition will be widespread. But if they are resolved, what might be wrong with creating a child using genetic material from three or more people, or from only two men, or only two women? In a world already familiar with the distinction between "genetic" parents and "social" parents, with step-dads, and with families that have two mommies, why does every child have a right to have been created from the "union" of one man and one woman? Is such a right really necessary to protect the welfare of children?

Fukuyama and Furger are right to draw our attention to the well-being of children in assisted reproduction, but I believe they are wrong to think that having a different kind of genetic origin necessarily causes harm. Unless we tell children that, due to *how* they were created, they are flawed or incomplete persons, what will really matter is that these children are loved and cared for by a nurturing family. They have a right to be fed, clothed, treated with dignity, and protected from harm—they even, I think, have a right to be (or a strong interest in being) told the truth about their genetic origins. But they don't have a right to have been created from the genetic material of only one man and one woman. To insist otherwise is to pull us back to a time when one's genetic origins determined one's worth.

7

Genetically Designing Babies Is Ethical Under Certain Circumstances

Patrick Tucker

Patrick Tucker is senior editor of the Futurist, *an international consumer magazine that explores social and technological trends.*

Technologies that allow parents to make genetic interventions that protect their children from disease and even bestow desired traits are not inherently unethical. In fact, valuable medical interventions such as vaccines involve genetic changes that protect children from deadly viruses and bacteria. Rather than dismiss genetically designed babies outright, policy makers can apply basic ethical principles to distinguish between ethical and unethical genetic interventions. For example, ethical genetic interventions should be as safe as natural reproduction, be used for the best interest of children, and not increase inequality.

Genomic research has been on a sprint since 2003, when researchers with the International Human Genome Project completed their map of the nucleotides that form human DNA. Some researchers believe that in the next few years, science will be able to recognize and possibly eliminate most of the world's congenital diseases (through a process called preimplantation genetic diagnosis, or PGD) and better treat many other diseases at the cellular level.

Patrick Tucker, "Genetic Ethics and 'Superbabies': Drawing the Line Between Preventing Ailments and Bestowing Advantages," *Futurist*, vol. 42, January–February 2008, p. 18.

Genomics may also enable otherwise healthy individuals to change their own DNA to improve athletic prowess or brain power, or allow the wealthy to artificially conceive genetically "superior" offspring. As new gene treatment options spring into existence, many people are seeking the line between legitimate gene therapy and superhuman enhancement.

" . . . Vaccinations make us superhumans, but no one ridicules enhancements of this sort."

A History of Enhancement

"The conceptual problem arises the moment we consider that some of our most valuable medical interventions are enhancements," writes bioethicist Ronald M. Green in *Babies by Design: The Ethics of Genetic Choice.* "Vaccines are a leading example. Almost no one is naturally immune to smallpox, polio, measles, whooping cough, or any of the other diseases that we vaccinate against.

"When we are inoculated, the DNA in our white blood cells undergoes irreversible genetic changes, initiating the synthesis of antibodies to many viruses and bacteria. Vaccinations make us superhumans, but no one ridicules enhancements of this sort. In most places in the United States and other industrialized countries, a child cannot enter school unless he or she is vaccinated," Green points out.

There are several types of genetic enhancement, each with its own ethical, and practical, strengths and weaknesses.

Somatic gene modification involves treating or changing the adult genes in a patient. A hypothetical example of somatic enhancement would be gene doping, in which an athlete takes a substance to "trick" his DNA into producing more testosterone on a regular basis.

Alternatively, germline gene modification is done before birth, usually during the embryo stage. A germline therapy for immunodeficiency could involve removing the sickle cell anemia gene from a developing embryo. One example of germline enhancement would be imbuing a developing embryo with certain characteristics seen as desirable, thus "designing a baby."

Somatic therapy is the less controversial of the two. Many researchers believe it holds the most promise, though meaningful breakthroughs in somatic therapy are still several years away.

Germline therapy may be more practically achievable. According to the Johns Hopkins Genetics and Public Policy Center, PGD has been used to screen for 1,000 genetic disorders. The therapy is also more provocative.

"I have been in the gene therapy field since 1987," says Dr. Markus Grompe, a fellow at the conservative Westchester Institute for Ethics and the Human Person. "It was very clear from day one that [genomics] could be used to change our species genetically by manipulating the germ line, i.e. making transgenic humans. There has been a consensus from day one that this would be off limits, ethically." Leon Kass, head of the President's Council on Bioethics has likewise argued against tampering with the human genome.

Millions . . . will likely turn to genetic science to help safeguard their children against disease, confer desired traits, or even imbue their offspring with physical or mental advantages.

The Ethical Questions

Inoculating children in the womb against serious diseases or disorders is not, on its face, controversial. But is manipulating cells to guard against traits that are merely undesirable ethical or unethical? Who gets to draw the boundary? As Green points out in his book, physical unattractiveness, or even plainness, can have real consequences over the course of human lifetime in terms of lost status and earning power. Is homeliness a disorder that should be treated genetically? What about being of a certain sex? The Mastertons, a British family, made headlines in the United Kingdom when they appealed to the government's Human Fertilisation and Embryology Authority for the right to determine the sex of their offspring by screening the fertilized eggs to be implanted. The Authority denied the request. Couples in the United States can use PGD to screen their baby's sex without restriction.

Babies by Design suggests four basic principles for distinguishing between gene manipulation that is ethical and that which is somewhat less than scrupulous.

1. *Genetic interventions should always be aimed at what is reasonably in the child's best interests.* "A child's likely consent is a rough-and-ready first test," writes Green, "but it should always be measured against the broader standard of what the larger community regards as being reasonably in the child's best interests."

2. *Genetic interventions should be almost as safe as natural reproduction.* According to Green, parents' wishes are an important part of the moral equation in determining what is ethical and what isn't. These wishes, he says, "have weight and should be respected so long as the child is not likely to be seriously harmed. . . . Where enhancement is concerned, we should factor into our thinking the prospect of added benefit for the child. If rational adults can invite some risks in undergoing cosmetic plastic surgery or a laser eye procedure, parents can also accept some added risk for their future child to give these benefits."

3. *We should avoid and discourage interventions that confer only "positional" advantage.* "Some requests for gene enhancements, like sports doping, could produce a tragedy

of the commons," argues Green. "Parents seeking a sports champion might try to have a child with an elevated red blood cell function. At its extreme, this request could significantly increase the child's risk of heart disease. Once many other parents started doing the same thing, the result would be no competitive advantage for anyone—bought at the price of increased health risks for all."

4. *Genetic interventions should not reinforce or increase unjust inequality and discrimination, economic inequality, or racism.* "Gene enhancements could widen the gap between the haves and the have-nots," Green points out. "We should think of effective ways of either controlling or increasing access to them."

Regardless of whatever guidelines governments enact, individuals frightened by the potential of gene science—or offended by the mere notion of it—will surely persist in the belief that the human genome is too precious to be tampered with. Yet, millions of others will likely turn to genetic science to help safeguard their children against disease, confer desired traits, or even imbue their offspring with physical or mental advantages. Just as the science of genetic manipulation is only in its infancy today, so the debate about what constitutes ethical genetic enhancement has barely begun.

Genetically Designing Babies Is Unethical

Michael Sandel

Michael Sandel, professor of political philosophy at Harvard University, is author of The Case Against Perfection: Ethics in the Age of Genetic Engineering.

Using genetic engineering to design babies that meet their parents' wishes is unethical. Indeed, designing babies is part of a growing problem in which parents try to exert increasing control over the lives of their children. Genetic intervention removes from parenting the humility that helps parents learn to live with the unexpected. In addition, designing children would decrease the sense of solidarity with those less fortunate: people would see the children of those who decide not to seek genetic advantages as unfit rather than as disadvantaged. Genetically altering human nature rather than making political and social improvements is an ethical defeat.

There's a growing debate about what limits, if any, should be put on genetic engineering. We are on a path in which in the not-too-distant future scientists and technicians will be able to select genes and may be able to shape characteristics of your children. Some people already argue that using that to select the sex of your child is fine, or perhaps for medical reasons. But what about other features? What if we could choose their hair color and type, their eye colors, their sexual orientation, their level of intelligence, their musical or writing ability or sports, dance, or artistic aptitude?

The Dark History of Eugenics

There is a long tradition that defends eugenics [a philosophy advocating the improvement of hereditary traits through selective breeding] in the name of "lifting up." Now we know that the eugenics movement has a very dark history, though it was a very respectable movement in the early part of the twentieth century. Eugenics was discredited by the Nazis, by genocide, the Nuremburg Laws, by the forced sterilization laws that were enacted by the majority of American states in the 1920s and 1930s. Yet, in its earlier days, eugenics was endorsed and embraced by social reformers, by American progressives: Theodore Roosevelt was a great supporter of eugenics, Margaret Sanger, who began Planned Parenthood, was a defender of eugenics. Oliver Wendell Holmes, in a famous Supreme Court case *Buck v. Bell*, upheld a forced sterilization law, with the notorious line that "three generations of imbeciles is enough." Oliver Wendell Holmes! So eugenics has a very respectable lineage if you look at the people who supported it, and yet it led to forced sterilization. It ultimately leads to genocide, even though it was first done in the name of those who have been burdened or disadvantaged.

What's the moral of the story of the dark history of eugenics? Some say it's that eugenics, in its earlier version, was coercive. State laws mandated sterilization in the so-called "feeble-minded," or in the criminal classes, and, of course, in Hitler's genocide. There are many today who say the only thing wrong with eugenics was its coerciveness, and if we could imagine a eugenic program that was not mandated by the State, that was not coercive, but was chosen by the individual parents trying to help and lift up their children, then there's nothing wrong with eugenics.

But I think that's a mistake. I think that coercion was not the only thing wrong with eugenics. What we have today with designer children is privatized eugenics, free market eugenics, individualistic eugenics. Without the broad social ambitions for everyone, it's really now an instrument for privileged parents to give their kids a competitive edge. Privatized eugenics reflect a deflation of the ideal of eugenics, perverse as that ideal was in its enactment, because it's no longer trying to uplift humanity, or entire societies, but just trying to get a competitive edge. I think what's wrong with eugenics, beyond coercion, is the fact of its ambition to try to control or exercise dominion over the genetic traits of the next generation. That's morally troubling, whether done on a society-wide basis or done by individual parents trying to give their kids a competitive edge.

Of course, there are objections about whether doing this can be made safe and predictable. And there is another question about making it available in a fair way, so that it would not only be an option for rich people. But what would be your objection if the designer child were an equal option for all, publicly subsidized as part of a universal health care system, and it could be done in a way that was safe and predictable?

The drive to create children of a certain character reflects an aspiration . . . to exercise our human will and our ability to remake human nature to serve our purposes and satisfy our desires.

Creating Children to Satisfy Our Desires

Is there a moral objection to this genetic engineering, beyond safety, beyond fairness? After all, we tend to praise parents who give their children every advantage they can: offer them music lessons to learn an instrument, play catch with them to learn how to be coordinated in sports, help them do their homework so that they can more fully learn what they need to learn. So what's the objection to parents wanting to give their children the advantage of genes that make it easier for them to succeed in creating a pleasant life for themselves?

It seems to me that there is a reason for a set of moral considerations that go beyond safety and fairness. What makes us most uneasy about the use of genetic engineering to enhance or to create something, has to do with the fact that the drive to create children of a certain character reflects an aspiration to freedom, mastery, and control, and to exercise our human will and our ability to remake human nature to serve our purposes and satisfy our desires. It seems to me there is something flawed but deeply attractive about that.

To appreciate children as gifts is to accept them as they come, not as products of our design or instruments of our ambition.

This uneasiness, I believe, connects to a recognition that there is a way in which who we are is a gift from the universe. And this is to say that not everything we are is a product of our own doing, and not everything in the world is open to any use we might desire or devise.

An appreciation of the giftedness of life might induce in us a certain humility. What I'm trying to articulate here is, in part, a religious sensibility, but its resonance reaches beyond religion.

Let's go back to the example of designer children. It's very hard to make sense of what's precious or special about the relationship between parents and children without drawing, at least a little, on the ethic of giftedness. To appreciate children as gifts is to accept them as they come, not as products of our design or instruments of our ambition. Parental love is not contingent, or at least it shouldn't be contingent, on attributes that the child happens to have. We choose our friends and our spouses at least partly on qualities that we find attractive, but we do not choose our children—that's an important moral fact about parenting. Even the most conscientious parent cannot be held wholly responsible for the child that they had. This is why parenting teaches us what the theologian William May calls "an openness to the unbidden."

The Hubris of Designing Children

The problem of genetic engineering lies in the hubris of the designing parents. Even if this disposition doesn't make parents tyrants to their children, still it disfigures the relation between parent and child and it deprives the parent of the humility, the human sympathies, and the openness to the unbidden.

Now, to appreciate children as gifts and blessings from God is not to be passive in the face of illness. It's true that medical treatment intervenes with nature, but it does so for the sake of health. It doesn't represent the same bid for mastery. Even strenuous medicine, to treat or cure diseases, doesn't constitute a Promethean assault. Medicine is at least governed by a certain norm, the norm of preserving and restoring, and that is what constitutes good health.

What counts as "good health" is open to argument. There is research about whether deafness or other disabilities should be cured, or if they should be part of an identity that is cherished. But even then, the disagreement comes from the assumption that the purpose of medicine is to promote health and cure disease.

Now there is a complexity with this idea of resisting the temptation to manage, direct, and protect our children. Because we do that as parents. Parents want to educate their children, give them every opportunity, help them learn an instrument, develop athletic skill. . . . What then is the difference, and this is not an easy question to answer, but what is the difference between providing help with health and training, and providing this help with the use of genetic enhancement? Parents spend all this money educating their children and giving them special advantages. If that's accurate, why isn't it equally as admirable for parents to use whatever genetic technology has been developed, provided it's safe, to enhance their children's chance at life, to give them a competitive edge?

The problem of genetic engineering lies in the hubris of the designing parents.

The Problem of Hyperparenting

The answer I would give to this question is that the defenders of genetic engineering are right to say that there is not such a bright line between the use of genetic technology to enhance children, and the kind of heavily managed, high-pressure child rearing practices that are common these days. But this similarity, this parallel, does not vindicate genetic enhancement. To the contrary, it highlights a problem with the high-pressure hyper-parenting tendencies that we see in our society today. We see the frenzy of parents at soccer game sidelines or at Little League. It is a frenzy, or an anxiety even, of the parents to manage, to hold, to direct their children's lives. I don't think there is such a clear line between these two practices, but this suggests that the overreaching in genetic parenting may actually shed light on the kind of overreaching frenzied parenting that we see now.

So, let me say a word about the larger moral stance if the account I have given is right. Some people would say of this drive for mastery and life control: "That's parents exercising their freedom to give their kids the best, and who are we to criticize that freedom?"

What would happen if biotechnology dissolved our sense of giftedness? There are two answers to this question. One of them is the religious answer (which suggests that using biotechnology has us assume a role in creation that seeks to make us on par with God). Biotechnology is, in a sense, "playing God."

The moral stakes can also be understood in secular terms. One way of seeing this is to consider what would be the effect on our moral landscape if the practice of designer parents became the common way of parenting? At least two key features of our moral culture would be transformed. One of them is humility and the other is solidarity.

Parents should be able to choose what they want to do, but they shouldn't be free to choose the burden of choice that this new technology creates.

Living with the Unexpected

Let me say a word about humility and why it matters as a social ethic. Parenthood is a school for humility. We care deeply about our children but cannot choose the kind we want. Humility teaches us to reign in our need for control and to live with the unexpected. One of the blessings of seeing ourselves as creatures of nature or God is that we are not always responsible for the way we are. The more we become masters of our genetics the greater burden we bear for the talents we have and the way we perform. So with the erosion of humility comes an explosion of responsibility.

Consider the use of genetic testing. In the past, giving birth to a child with Down syndrome was a matter of chance. Today, parents of children with Down syndrome are judged or blamed. Because people will say to them "why did you bring this child into the world?" So the responsibility is greater because we have a choice. Parents should be able to choose what they want to do, but they shouldn't be free to choose the burden of choice that this new technology creates.

A Diminished Sense of Solidarity

Along with the explosion of responsibility over our own fate and that of our children, comes, paradoxically, a diminished sense of solidarity with those less fortunate than ourselves. Here's why: the more open we are to chance in the control over our own success, the more reason we have to share our fate with others. Why, after all, do the successful owe anything to the least advantaged members of society? The answers to these questions lie very heavily in the notions of giftedness. They lean on the idea that our success has nothing to do with hard work, or other things within our control, but on good fortune—the result of the genetic lottery. If we regard our genetics as gifts rather than achievements for which we can claim credit, then we have no basis to claim that we are entitled to the good things in society.

> *Rather than increase our genetic powers to fit ourselves into society, we should . . . create political and social realms that are more hospitable . . . to the limitations of imperfect human beings.*

A lively sense of the contingency of our gifts can be used in a "meritocratic" society like ours to prevent us from sliding into the idea that the rich are rich because they are more deserving than the poor. If genetic engineering enabled us to override the results of the genetic lottery, if it enabled us to replace chance with choice, it's likely that the gifted character of human powers and achievements would recede, and with it, perhaps, our capacity to see ourselves as sharing a common fate. The successful would be even more likely than they are now to see themselves as self-made and self-sufficient, and those at the bottom of society would be seen not as disadvantaged, but simply as unfit. The meritocracy would become less forgiving. So that's why humility and solidarity as features of our moral culture can help us preserve a lively sense of gifted-ness of our nature, of our talents, and of our achievements. . . .

So, to go back to the question with which I began, beyond safety and beyond fairness, what is the source of our unease about designer children? I think it has something to do with our big questions about human nature and the limits of the Promethean project of mastery and control. It is tempting to think that bioengineering our children and selves is an exercise in freedom, but it really isn't. Because changing our nature to fit the world rather than the other way around is actually an ethical defeat. It distracts us from reflecting critically on the world. It deadens the impulse for social and political improvement. So rather than increase our genetic powers to fit ourselves into society, we should do what we can to create political and social realms that are more hospitable to the gifts and also to the limitations of imperfect human beings.

9

Gender Selection Is Ethical

Norbert Gleicher and David H. Barad

Norbert Gleicher, professor of obstetrics, gynecology, and reproductive sciences at Yale University School of Medicine, is a consultant at the Center for Human Reproduction. David H. Barad is professor of epidemiology and social medicine at Albert Einstein College of Medicine in the Bronx, New York.

In developed nations such as the United States, gender selection is not inherently unethical. Research suggests that while there is a greater demand for male than female babies among those parents who choose to select gender in the United States, the bias disappears when certain ethic groups are removed from the analysis. This finding contradicts the assumption that gender selection always discriminates against females. Thus, adopting ethical opinions concerning gender selection that apply to all cultures worldwide is unfair. Women who meet objective criteria and have not been coerced should be allowed to choose the gender of their children.

Elective gender selection has remained controversial worldwide. In the United States (US), the issue had remained largely dormant until the Ethics Committee of the American Society for Reproductive Medicine (ASRM) published an opinion, potentially validating elective gender selection under selected circumstances. This publication gave rise to controversy in the US, matching differences of opinion elsewhere in the world.

Norbert Gleicher and David H. Barad, "The Choice of Gender: Is Elective Gender Selection, Indeed, Sexist?" *Human Reproduction*, vol. 22, November 1, 2007, pp. 3038–41.

A Variety of Ethical Opinions

Some ethics opinions (from major professional societies) have differentiated between 'pre-fertilization' gender selection by sperm sorting, and 'post-fertilization' sex selection through *in vitro* fertilization (IVF) and preimplantation genetic diagnosis (PGD), with the former considered more ethically acceptable than the latter. The reasons are complex, with many ethicists considering the creation of a human embryo as a differentiating step. A recently issued opinion by the Ethics Committee of the American College of Obstetricians and Gynecologists (ACOG), however, placed a surprising degree of emphasis on a different argument: in following the reasoning of the International Federation of Gynecology and Obstetrics, it considers all forms of elective gender selection as discriminatory and sexist.

The introduction of elective gender selection would, at least in the developed world, not affect gender ratios to a significant degree.

In its opinion, the ACOG committee states, 'The committee shares the concerns expressed by the United Nations and the International Federation of Gynecology and Obstetrics that sex selection can be motivated by and reinforce the devaluation of women'. Continuing, the committee concluded that, '. . .the use of sex selection techniques for family balancing violates the norm of equality between the sexes; moreover, this ethical objection arises regardless of the timing of the selection (i.e. preconception or postconception) or the stage of development of the embryo or fetus.'

Such an implied utilization of elective gender selection for sexist and discriminatory purposes, devaluatory to women, of course implies that, given the opportunity, a large majority of couples would choose gender selection for male offspring. This contention has been disputed on theoretical grounds, and based on population surveys, but still has led to international regulatory and legal prohibitions, although, in an exception, the House of Commons Science and Technology Committee of the United Kingdom recently adopted less dogmatic recommendations.

Studying Gender Selection

The issue has, however, never before objectively been investigated. This study attempts such an investigation in a multiethnic US patient population, which chose to undergo gender selection procedures for family balancing purposes. . . .

The results of this study demonstrate overall a statistically larger demand for male than female gender selection. When these data are, however, further analyzed, it becomes apparent that the demand for males is driven by strong biases toward male selection in only some ethnic minorities. Except for Chinese, Arab/Muslim and Asian-Indian patients, no other ethnic group demonstrates a bias toward male selection. Indeed, the opposite is true, especially among Caucasian/Hispanic patients, where 59.6% of selections were for female. This finding confirms previously expressed opinions, and population surveys in a number of countries, which have argued that the introduction of elective gender selection would, at least in the developed world, not affect gender ratios to a significant degree.

In the US, two prior surveys have addressed this issue: [T.] Jain *et al.* noted a significant preference for female gender, especially in older women, who were not religious, had more living children, had only sons and carried a diagnosis of male factor infertility. Interestingly, nulliparous [never having given birth] women, who, of course, were not the subject of our study, did not demonstrate preference for the selection of one gender over the other. Among parous [having given birth] women, the distribution of gender among their children significantly affected their preferred choices: those with only daughters preferred to select for male; those with only sons preferred selection for female, thus validating the concept of family balancing.

[E.] Dahl *et al.* noted that 50% of men and women wished to have a balanced family, 7% wanted more boys, 6% more girls, 5% with only boys, 4% with only girls and 27% had no preference.

Our study did not demonstrate that age represented a contributing factor toward the differences observed between ethnic groups. Asian patients were, however, minimally younger than non-Asian and younger age predisposed to male selection. Especially remarkable was the fact that the two most committed ethnic groups, Caucasian/Hispanic (to female selection) and Chinese (to male selection), were almost identical in mean ages.

The Contradicting Arguments

This study also contradicts the argument that offering elective gender selection for family balancing purposes 'always' is discriminatory against females and should, therefore, 'always' be considered sexist, as expressed by the United Nations, a recent ACOG Ethics Opinion and in a number of ethical opinions in the literature. The data presented here instead suggest that in the US, the situation is more complex: although certain minorities may still have maintained cultural biases of their homelands, a majority of remaining couples do not demonstrate discriminatory, or sexist, behavior toward females. Indeed, this majority may actually act discriminatorily against males by predominantly selecting for female. Discrimination against male gender has, however, to our best knowledge, never been recognized by any of the international ethical panels commenting on this issue.

This study does not address the potential choice [of] gender [that] couples would prefer in first pregnancies. Although the studies by Jain *et al.* and Dahl *et al.* suggest that expected findings should not differ significantly from those reported in this study, such a conclusion remains to be confirmed by future studies in the field.

Studying Ethnic Minorities

As a New York based fertility center, our program appears well suited to investigate this issue because many of our patients represent ethnic minorities, where, for cultural reasons, gender discrimination in favor of male selection can, indeed, be expected. The 22 Chinese, 6 Arab/Muslim and 6 Asian-Indian couples, who to a significant degree favored male selection, represent the approximate overall representations of these ethnic groups within our center's patient population. It is, therefore, reassuring that the availability of gender section for family balancing purposes does not appear to have selectively drawn couples from these two minorities.

In the US, ethnic minorities are usually concentrated in large urban centers. For example, Chinese minorities can be found in largest numbers in New York City and San Francisco areas, whereas Arab/Muslim populations concentrate in the New York City and Michigan areas. The ethnic biases presented here toward male gender selection will, therefore, only be visible in relatively small parts of the country.

The offer of elective gender selection for family balancing purposes does not necessarily violate the norm of equality between the sexes to the disfavor of females.

Other minorities were represented in only small sample sizes, and lack of obvious biases can, therefore, not necessarily be understood as absence of such biases. Further studies, involving larger patient populations, are needed to fully absolve other minority populations from anti-female biases.

At the same time, this study also suggests that in a less ethnically diverse population, representing a more homogenous Caucasian/Hispanic population, and thus a large majority of the US population, one, indeed, can expect no bias toward male selections and, potentially, even bias toward the selection of females.

Drawing Conclusions

This observation suggests that in an ethnically diverse, and economically developed country, like the US, the offer of elective gender selection for family balancing purposes does not necessarily violate the norm of equality between the sexes to the disfavor of females, as suggested in the recent Ethics Opinion of ACOG, and, therefore, does not universally appear to represent a discriminatory and sexist medical practice.

In developed countries ethnic biases [in favor of male selection] will fade over time as new generations are influenced by their new homeland's cultural habits.

Yet, at the same time these findings raise the question [of] how obviously existing biases toward male gender selection in certain minority populations should be addressed. We have given considerable thought to this issue but have been unable to reach an unequivocal answer: on the one hand, we strongly believe in the right of patients to choose the makeup of their families; however, our belief in such rights is, of course, predicated on free choice for each individual, which in an enlightened society will, as most published data and this study have demonstrated, lead to an approximately equal gender distribution, not discriminatory toward females. When such free choice, based on ethnic habits and/or pressures, is lacking, it would seem only fair to withhold the right to choose the gender makeup of one's family. The decision to withhold the right of elective gender selection would, therefore, appear appropriate in countries where widespread discrimination against females, indeed, exists.

Moral and ethical values, however, vary in different societies and, as this study demonstrated, in different ethnicities within US society. It would, therefore, appear mistaken to assume that universal ethics opinion can be developed for worldwide consumption, as suggested by the United Nations' opinion on elective gender selection, and by some individuals. Instead, developed nations would be well advised to develop educational outreach programs for their ethnic minorities, which teach non-discriminatory value systems, while allowing the conduct of practices which are not abused by a large majority of the population.

It seems reasonable to assume that in developed countries ethnic biases will fade over time as new generations are influenced by their new homeland's cultural habits. Our experience with elective gender selection also indicates that, independent of ethnicity, the choice to pursue this process is in over 80% of couples initiated by the woman. In developed countries, with mixed ethnic populations, like the US, this observation suggests that a psychological investigation, prior to initiation of treatment, may allow for an objective differentiation between women who chose gender selection out of free will, and those who feel coerced. Such a psychological examination could then, in a non-discriminatory way, be used to determine who should, and who should not, be given access to selective gender determination of their offspring.

We in that sense agree with Dahl who commented that outlawing a harmless practice in one country, simply because it has been demonstrated to have potentially harmful effects elsewhere in the world, represents bad public policy. Similarly, there is no reason to impose ethics opinions on a whole nation, simply because a small minority acts in an unethical fashion. Ethical advisories should, in their respective opinions, be more considerate of national value systems, and should not attempt to find consensus based on lowest common denominators.

10

Gender Selection Can in Some Cases Be Unethical

Preeti Shekar

Preeti Shekar is a feminist activist and journalist from India.

The decision to select a child's gender may be harmful if made for social rather than medical reasons. In societies that favor male children, gender selection technologies help parents to select male rather than female offspring. This helps the parents avoid resorting to female infanticide and feticide and removes pressure on the mother from husband and relatives to bear sons. However, use of these technologies for gender selection for societal reasons perpetuates sexist attitudes about the feminine gender. Moreover, the practice creates an imbalance in the ratio of males to females in countries, such as India and China, that favor the use of these gender selection methods.

Nobel Prize–winning economist Amartya Sen speaks of "missing women." Other experts call the phenomenon "gendercide." They refer to gender selection, a practice that is thriving in South Asian societies in the United States and abroad, thanks to new, sophisticated reproductive technologies.

"We get several calls a week from folks, especially from India and China either living here or who plan to visit, asking if we can definitely help them make a baby boy," notes a hotline operator for The Fertility Institutes in Los Angeles, one of numerous clinics that have mushroomed in the United States to cater to the growing demand for state-of-the-art reproductive technologies.

Doctors Use Three Techniques

There are currently three techniques of gender selection available: pre-natal testing, pre-implantation genetic diagnoses and sperm sorting. Pre-natal testing consists of ultrasound that detects the gender of the fetus, allowing parents to abort if the fetus is of an undesired sex. The latter two techniques are more complex. With genetic diagnosing, a woman first goes through in vitro fertilization, during which her eggs are surgically extracted and fertilized outside the body. Doctors then test the embryos and implant only those of the desired gender. Originally developed for the detection of sex-linked genetic disorders, the technique is now employed in gender selection. MicroSort technology, or sperm sorting, involves literally sorting through sperm to find the sex-determining chromosome (Y for a boy and X for a girl) and then inseminating the woman with sperm that will create a baby of the desired gender.

Gender selection technologies are of increasing interest to an elite class that filters issues through a paradigm of choice and access. While many mainstream news reports and articles do gently hint at the ethical issues of using the technologies for non-medical purposes, the final verdict rests on each family's shoulders. Since genetic diagnosing and sperm sorting help families avoid the trauma of female infanticide and feticide that earlier, less sophisticated technologies allowed, it is a popular notion, even among some progressive members of the South Asian community. What's lacking, however, is a deeper analysis of the sexist and racist consequences of the technologies.

"It is important to have a critical discussion of the implications of reproductive technologies, especially for women of color," affirms Sujatha Jesudason of the Center for Genetics and Society, who is a veteran reproductive rights activist and community organizer. "Because if we don't, then we as a society let the market determine what is acceptable instead of challenging the current and future misuse of technology that is growing increasingly sophisticated. This is a deeply ethical and feminist issue."

South Asians Are Targeted

Despite the formidable costs—between $18,000 and $23,000 on average—it is not uncommon for middle-class and affluent couples from India and China to visit the United States to access these technologies, which are either banned or unavailable back home.

Dubbed as the new face of reproductive tourism, many clinics encourage the practice with slick marketing strategies targeting South Asian communities. Advertisements for gender selection appear in Asia-bound in-flight magazines and increasingly in South Asian community papers. Often, the new technologies are framed in "neutral" ways (many U.S.-based institutes refer to gender selection as "family balancing"), reducing the practice to the level of the family's choice to have a baby boy or girl.

Perhaps the most disturbing aspect underlying the availability of these technologies is the racism that helps perpetuate it. In their newsletters and online testimonials, the Washington, D.C-based Genetics and IVF Institute and The Fertility Institutes with centers in L.A., Las Vegas and Mexico, feature largely white American couples who herald the technology for enabling them to complete their families. The fact that Asian families use these technologies to sire boys is completely suppressed. While clinic websites project availability and access as a race-neutral phenomenon, the news reports featuring these centers and calls to their information hotlines paint a different picture—one in which representatives grudgingly acknowledge that Asian couples are a huge consumer base that typically prefers boys.

A 2006 UNICEF report finds India battling a highly skewed national gender ratio of 927 females for every 1,000 males—a drop from the 1991 figure of 945 females for every 1,000 males.

Most of the calls to centers like The Fertility Institutes are from women. There is enormous pressure on women from their families and husbands to produce that baby boy who will continue the family name and be their future economic savior. "A lot of women who come to us for help tell us that the sex of their baby determines the security of their married life," says Atashi Chakravarty, who heads Narika, a Bay Area-based group that works to end domestic violence in the South Asian community. "Giving birth to a girl can many times accelerate the abuse and violence they experience from their husband or his family."

A Worldwide Issue

As profits of these U.S.-based clinics soar, several South Asian governments have become alarmed at the imbalanced gender ratios in India and China, where "son preference" is an established reality. A 2006 UNICEF report finds India battling a highly skewed national gender ratio of 927 females for every 1,000 males—a drop from the 1991 figure of 945 females for every 1,000 males. China is experiencing a similarly alarming imbalance that is compounded by its one-child-per-family policy. But this hasn't stopped the Genetics and IVF Institute from operating branches in Shanghai and Guangzhou since 1996.

Numbers a[s]ide, the concerns of reproductive rights groups and activists worldwide focus on the ethics of gender selection. These concerns caused Canada, Australia and the United Kingdom to ban the use of reproductive technology for gender selection purposes. But in the United States, the clinics propagate it as free choice.

As new technologies emerge that enable a booming middle class in South Asian countries to access them freely and guilt-lessly, activists, community organizers and policymakers are recognizing the need to work across borders and boundaries.

11

Disposing of Unused Frozen Embryos Poses Ethical Challenges

Liza Mundy

Liza Mundy, a staff writer at the Washington Post, *is author of* Everything Conceivable, *a book that explores the issues surrounding reproductive technology.*

The number of frozen in vitro fertilization (IVF) embryos is growing. How to dispose of them poses ethical challenges for many IVF patients. Some are concerned about giving unused frozen embryos to other infertile couples, who would be creating biological siblings unknown to the donor family. Another option is to donate the embryos for scientific research, which for some raises questions of whether embryos are human lives or simply cells. For parents who once viewed these cells as potential children, the shift to thinking of embryos as cells is difficult. Unfortunately, fertility clinics offer little or no counseling on this decision.

Janis Elspas is a mother of four. Unlike most parents, she had three of her children simultaneously. The nine-year-old triplets were born in 1997 after Elspas underwent a series of in vitro fertilization [IVF] treatments for infertility. Her oldest child, 10, is the happy result of a prior IVF treatment round. Elspas worked hard to get her children, and is grateful to have them. But four, thanks very much, are plenty. The problem is

Liza Mundy, "Souls on Ice: America's Embryo Glut and the Wasted Promise of Stem Cell Research," *Mother Jones*, July 1, 2006. Copyright © 2006 Foundation for National Progress. Reproduced by permission.

that Elspas also has 14 embryos left over from the treatment that produced her 10-year-old. The embryos are stored in liquid nitrogen at a California frozen storage facility—she is not entirely sure where—while Elspas and her husband ponder what to do with them.

It seems fair to estimate that by now the number of embryos in limbo in the United States alone is closer to half a million.

Give them away to another couple, to gestate and bear? Her own children's full biological siblings—raised in a different family? Donate them to scientific research? Let them . . . finally . . . lapse? It is, she and her husband find, an intractable problem, one for which there is no satisfactory answer. So what they have done—thus far—is nothing. Nothing, that is, but agonize.

"I don't have the heart to thaw them," says Elspas, who works as media relations director for a multi-birth networking group called the Triplet Connection. "But then again, I don't have the will to do something with them."

Embryos in Limbo

Elspas is by no means alone, either in having frozen human embryos she and her husband must eventually figure out what to do with, or in the moral paralysis she feels, surveying the landscape of available choices. In fact, she is part of an explosively growing group. In 2002, the Society for Assisted Reproductive Technology—the research arm for U.S. fertility doctors—decided to find out how many unused embryos had accumulated in the nation's 430 fertility clinics. The Rand consulting group, hired to do a head count, concluded that 400,000 frozen embryos existed—a staggering number, twice as large as previous estimates. Given that hundreds of thousands of IVF treatment rounds have since been performed, it seems fair to estimate that by now the number of embryos in limbo in the United States alone is closer to half a million.

This embryo glut is forcing many people to reconsider whatever they thought they thought about issues such as life and death and choice and reproductive freedom. It's a dilemma that has been quietly building: The first American IVF baby was born in 1981, less than a decade after *Roe v. Wade* was decided. Thanks in part to *Roe*, fertility medicine in this country developed in an atmosphere of considerable reproductive freedom (read: very little government oversight), meaning, among other things, that responsibility for embryo disposition rests squarely with patients. The number of IVF rounds, or "cycles," has grown to the point that in 2003 about 123,000 cycles were performed, to help some of the estimated 1 in 7 American couples who have difficulty conceiving naturally. Early on, it proved relatively easy to freeze a lab-created human embryo—which unlike, say, hamburger meat, can be frozen, and thawed, and refrozen, and thawed, and then used. (To be precise, the technical term is "pre-embryo," or "conceptus"; a fertilized egg is not considered an embryo until about two weeks of development, and IVF embryos are frozen well before this point.) Over time—as fertility drugs have gotten more powerful and lab procedures more efficient—it has become possible to coax more and more embryos into being during the average cycle. Moreover, as doctors transfer fewer embryos back into patients, in an effort to reduce multiple births, more of the embryos made are subsequently frozen.

And so, far from going away, the accumulation of human embryos is likely to grow, and grow, and grow. And in growing, the embryo overstock is likely to change—or at least complicate—the way we collectively think about human life at its earliest stages, and morally what is the right thing to do with it. At some point, embryos may alter or even explode the reproductive landscape: It is IVF embryos, after all, that are at the center of the nation's stem cell debate, which itself has prompted a new national conversation about life and reproductive liberty, creating new alliances as well as schisms. In 2001, as one of his first major domestic policy decisions, George W. Bush banned federal funding for labs developing new stem cell lines using leftover IVF embryos; then in May 2005, the U.S. House of Representatives passed a bill approving funding for stem cell research using these same embryos, setting the stage for an eventual conservative showdown. In the course of this debate, embryos have emerged as another tool for truly hardline conservatives looking for new ways to beat back abortion rights. Like "fetal rights" laws that seemingly protect unborn children from acts of homicide, "embryo rights" are being waved about as a weapon in the assault on abortion rights, as anti-abortion lawmakers talk about seizing control over frozen embryo stores; limiting the creation of new embryos; or both.

Deciding the fate of frozen embryos is known as the "disposition decision," and it is one of the hardest decisions patients face.

Reviving Questions About Life

But the impact of the embryo is also taking place on a more subtle and personal level. The glut's very existence illuminates how the newest reproductive technologies are complicating questions about life; issues that many people thought they had resolved are being revived and reconsidered, in a different emotional context. As with ultrasound technology—which permits parents to visualize a fetus in utero—IVF allows many patients to form an emotional attachment to a form of human life that is very early, it's true, but still life, and still human. People bond with photos of three-day-old, eight-cell embryos. They ardently wish for them to grow into children. The experience can be transforming: "I was like, 'I created these things, I feel a sense of responsibility for them,'" is how one IVF patient put it. Describing herself as staunchly pro-choice, this patient found that she could not rest until she located a person—actually, two people—willing to bring her excess embryos to term. The presence of embryos for whom (for which?) they feel a certain undefined moral responsibility presents tens of thousands of Americans with a dilemma for which nothing—nothing—has prepared them.

A new demographic is wrestling with questions initially posed by contraception and abortion. A world away from the exigencies, mitigating circumstances, and carefully honed ideologies that have grown up in and around U.S. abortion clinics, it is people like Janis Elspas who are being called upon to think, hard, about when life begins, and when it is—or is not—right to terminate it. They are in this position, ironically enough, not because they don't want a family, but precisely because they do. Among the nation's growing ranks of IVF patients, deciding the fate of frozen embryos is known as the "disposition decision," and it is one of the hardest decisions patients face, so unexpectedly problematic that many decide, in the end, to punt, a choice that is only going to make the glut bigger, the moral problem more looming and unresolved.

Surprising Attachments

To show just how difficult embryo disposition can be: Dr. Robert Nachtigall, a veteran San Francisco reproductive endocrinologist, directed a study of patients who had conceived using IVF together with egg donation, another rapidly growing niche of fertility medicine. As Nachtigall and his colleagues at the University of California, San Francisco were interviewing these parents, they were struck by comments made, separately, by several couples.

Hard as it was deciding whether to go ahead with egg donation, these parents said, it was harder still deciding the fate of their leftover embryos.

"Until recently, I don't know if any of us were aware of the scope of the embryo dilemma," Nachtigall told colleagues at the 2005 annual meeting held by the American Society for Reproductive Medicine (ASRM), the trade group for fertility doctors. Struck by these unprompted revelations, he and fellow researchers decided to do a new study, this one looking explicitly at the way patients think about their unused, iced-down embryos. The study was published in 2005 in the journal *Fertility and Sterility*. Strikingly, Nachtigall found that even in one of the bluest [most liberal] regions of the country, which is to say, among people living in and around San Francisco, few were able to view a three-day-old laboratory embryo with anything like detachment. "Parents variously conceptualized frozen embryos as biological tissue, living entities, 'virtual' children having interests that must be considered and protected, siblings of their living children, genetic or psychological 'insurance policies,' and symbolic reminders of their past infertility," his report noted. Many seemed afflicted by a kind of Chinatown syndrome, thinking of them simultaneously as: Children! Tissue! Children! Tissue!

Couples ... were confused yet deeply affected by the responsibility of deciding what to do with their embryos.

An earlier study, conducted by psychologist Susan Klock and colleagues at the Northwestern University School of Medicine, found that many patients begin IVF with some notion about how they will dispose of surplus embryos. (The choices come down to five: use them; donate them for research; donate them to another infertile person; freeze them indefinitely; or have them thawed, that is, quietly disposed of.) What Klock also reported was that many couples found their thinking transformed once treatment was over. More than half the couples who had planned to dispose of their embryos decided, instead, to use them, or donate them. Conversely, seven of the eight couples who had planned to donate them to research decided to use them, or dispose of them. Nearly all who had planned to donate their embryos to another couple found that, when push came to shove, they could not relinquish their potential genetic offspring. In short: Almost all reconsidered, not in any way that could be neatly summarized. All in all, 71 percent changed their minds about what to do. Also striking: Only about half of patients with embryos stored for more than three years could be located. The rest were incommunicado.

Many [couples] were troubled ... by the notion of donating embryos to research or to another couple, and thereby losing control over their fate and well-being.

A Torturous Decision

Nachtigall's study elaborated on these findings. Couples, he found, were confused yet deeply affected by the responsibility of deciding what to do with their embryos. They wanted to do the right thing. All of the 58 couples in his study had children as a result of treatment, so they knew, well, what even three-day-old embryos can and do grow into. (Nachtigall is currently studying a much larger sample of couples, where both egg and sperm come from the parents. It should answer the question of whether couples who use donor eggs are in any way distinct in their thinking about embryos.) "Some saw them as biological material, but most recognized the potential for life," Nachtigall told colleagues at the ASRM meeting. "For many couples, it seems there is no good decision; yet they still take it seriously morally."

For virtually all patients, he found, the disposition decision was torturous, the end result unpredictable. "Nothing feels right," he reported patients telling him. "They literally don't know what the right, the good, the moral thing is." In the fluid process of making a decision—any decision—some try to talk themselves into a clinical detachment. "Little lives, that's how I thought about them," said one woman. "But you have to switch gears and think, 'They're not lives, they're cells. They're science.' That's kind of what I had to switch to." Others were not able to make that switch, thinking of their embryos as almost sentient. "My husband talked about donating them to research, but there is some concern that this would not be a peaceful way to go," said one woman. Another said, "You start saying to yourself, 'Every one of these is potentially a life.'"

Many were troubled, Nachtigall said, by the notion of donating embryos to research or to another couple, and thereby losing control over their fate and well-being; they seemed to feel a parental obligation to protect their embryos. "I couldn't give my children to someone else to raise, and I couldn't give these embryos to someone else to bear," said one woman. Another woman described her embryos as a psychic insurance policy, providing "intangible solace" against the fundamental parental terror that an existing child might die. "What if [my daughter] got leukemia?" said yet another, who considered her frozen embryos a potential source of treatment. A patient put the same notion more bluntly: "You have the idea that in a warehouse somewhere there's a replacement part should yours get lost, or there is something wrong with them."

Uncommon Disposal Methods

For others, embryos carried a price tag that made them seem like a consumer good; a few parents considered destroying them to be a "waste" of all the money spent on treatment.

"You weigh what's best," Nachtigall quoted one parent as saying, but what's best is not, often, clear. This parent continued: "Are they people? Aren't they people? In part of my mind, they're potential people, but the point is, it seems odd to me to keep them frozen forever. It seems like not facing the issue."

A patient who had decided to donate embryos for research said, "We've agreed that it's the right thing for us to do, but the final step is to get the forms notarized, and we haven't done it. I will honestly say that it will be a day of mourning."

For those couples who did reach a decision, the resolution came as a great relief, bringing with it, his report noted, "a profound sense of completeness and resolution."

Nachtigall also found that patients sometimes disposed of embryos in novel ways that fell short of actual plug-pulling. In a version of the rhythm method of contraception [having sex only when the woman is infertile during her menstrual cycle], he learned, some patients (though none of the ones in his study) solved their dilemma through the laborious—and expensive—process of having leftover embryos transferred into the woman's uterus at a time in her monthly cycle when implantation would be unlikely. Others buried embryos. Still others could not bring themselves to dispose of them at all. "We'll have a couple more pregnancies and we'll just grow the whole lot," one father told Nachtigall and his team.

Of the 58 couples Nachtigall and his group interviewed, the average couple had seven frozen embryos in storage. The average embryo had been in storage for four years. Even after that much time had elapsed, 72 percent had not decided what to do, and a number echoed the words of one patient: "We can't talk about it." The embryos keep alive the question of whether to have more children, a topic on which many spouses disagree. "I still have six in the bank," said one woman, who had not given up the idea of bearing them. "They call to me. I hate to talk about it. But they call to me." Her words are reminiscent of a comment made by the singer Celine Dion, who, after undergoing IVF in 2001, later said, in describing her plans for a second child: "This frozen embryo that is in New York is my child waiting to be brought to life." . . .

An Unlikely Conversation

So what are we going to do with our embryo glut? Robert Nachtigall believes that with better patient counseling and logistical coordination between fertility clinics and research labs, many more unused embryos could be directed toward stem cell research, and that many patients would be happy to know that their embryos are being used to find a cure for afflictions such as Parkinson's disease and juvenile diabetes.

"I think it's a mistake to call it a glut," says Nachtigall. "I mean, these embryos are created in a process as hundreds of thousands of couples attempt to overcome infertility, and their presence is perhaps an unanticipated side effect of the use of advanced reproductive technology. But there is nothing inherently negative or wrong about their existence, and as we turn our attention to them, we may find that indeed they could be a tremendous resource for science, the country, and for mankind, for that matter."

The problem is few fertility clinics counsel patients about disposition, at least not at any length; and because of the ban on federal funding, few labs can receive human embryos for research. Nor has the fertility profession served itself or its patients entirely well, encouraging the idea that embryos *are* multicelled clumps of tissue.

They are multicelled clumps of tissue, it's true, but they are also more complicated and more emotionally fraught. One of the powerful findings of Nachtigall's study was how isolated patients felt in making the disposition decision; how they longed for counseling, advice, some sort of out-loud moral conversation between people who had been through, and thought through, the same issues. Whether the reproductive rights community might ever hold such a grand, collective conversation seems unlikely, in this charged political atmosphere. But it would be useful, to put it mildly.

Meanwhile, the technology itself is so new that nobody knows what the expiration date on embryos might be. Might all these embryos become nonviable and nonproblematic? Unlikely. Recently, a San Francisco woman gave birth using an embryo that had been frozen for 13 years. So patients like Janis Elspas continue to agonize over their aging embryonic stores. An Orthodox Jew, Elspas believes her religion would permit her to quietly terminate what are, basically, little more than fertilized eggs. "But considering all the pain and suffering we went through to get those embryos, I still consider it the destruction of a God-given gift."

After weighing all the options, and rejecting them, one patient says wryly, but a little wearily: "Maybe when I die, they'll just bury my embryos with me."

12

Freezing Eggs to Delay Motherhood Should Be Discouraged

Laura Vanderkam

Laura Vanderkam, author of Grindhopping: Build a Rewarding Career Without Paying Your Dues, *is a member of* USA Today's *board of contributors. Her work has also appeared in* Reader's Digest, Scientific American, *and* Wired.

The number of women choosing to delay motherhood is growing. However, freezing embryos to avoid the fertility problems that older women sometimes face is a poor solution. The egg-freezing process is costly and is not foolproof. The best way for women to ensure that they will be able to have a family is to do so when they are young. Raising children while furthering a career is indeed a challenge. However, the challenges remain whether a woman is young or old.

When Karen Soika . . . hit her late 30s, she made a lot of big decisions. She ended a relationship. She quit her job as a pharmaceutical executive. She applied to medical school. The one problem? Figuring out where children fit in this picture. "I didn't want to take the chance of being 45 and not having a child," she says.

Megan Griswold, 38, also had that realization a few years ago. This acupuncturist/writer was in a relationship, but her partner wasn't ready for kids, and she wasn't sure she was, either. "I think being a good mother means I'm mature and know my way in the world, so I can be helpful to a little boy or girl," she says. With her life in flux, but her biological clock ticking, Griswold debated what to do.

Soika and Griswold face an increasingly common dilemma. The percentage of 30- to 34-year-old American women who are single has roughly tripled over the past three decades. Others may be in relationships but spend too much of their 20s and 30s building—or switching—careers to focus on having kids until it's almost too late.

The best way to beat the clock is not to freeze your eggs, but to create a family when you're young and adapt your life to that reality.

A Unique Solution to a Common Dilemma

Although the dilemma is common, their solution is not. Both recently opted for "oocyte preservation"—freezing their eggs. This procedure, in which a woman's eggs are retrieved and stored so they can be fertilized and implanted, offered the tantalizing possibility of letting them have their biological children later, when their lives had settled down.

Extend Fertility, a company based in Massachusetts that helped Soika and Griswold, reports that about 200 women have frozen their eggs through their national network of clinics. Worldwide, only a few hundred babies have been born from the technology. Yet these small numbers have still set off an outsized howl in the debate over women's life choices. Many television network shows have featured the process. *Newsweek* called it the "greatest thing since birth control."

Start Young Instead

All the noise masks a harder truth: Egg freezing is still an expensive, elaborate and hardly foolproof way to have children.

The danger is that younger women will believe the hype and view the technology's existence as a reason not to worry about fertility until their lives are in order. That would be unfortunate because the best way to beat the clock is not to freeze your eggs, but to create a family when you're young and adapt your life to that reality. Most women already do this. There's no reason egg freezing's target market of educated professional women—those who can bend the world to their whims—can't figure this out as well.

No one denies that egg freezing is an exciting technology. Researchers have undertaken a near-Manhattan Project to improve the process, which was originally developed to help cancer patients facing treatment-induced infertility. The larger market, though, is thirtysomething women who, having watched their mothers flee the kitchen for the workforce, assumed that school and work were the hard parts. They took childbearing for granted and now are scrambling to create families before their fertility fails.

Egg freezing seems to offer an out, but there are cracks in this shell. For starters, egg freezing works best when eggs are retrieved at peak quality. For most women, this occurs when they're in their mid-20s. But few 25-year-olds feel the urgency to make such a decision, nor can they afford it if they do. Treatment can cost $10,000–$20,000. Storage fees also add up fast. And that's if the process works.

The American Society for Reproductive Medicine still considers the technology "experimental." Human eggs are frustratingly prone to freezer burn and must be harvested in batches of 10 or more to achieve statistical likelihood of creating a viable embryo. No one who has watched friends go through the grueling regimen of shots, drugs and daily doctor's visits that in vitro fertilization involves would think this is easy.

Never a "Best" Time

Many women who freeze their eggs realize this and would still prefer to have children the old-fashioned way. As Soika says, "I was ready to be barefoot and pregnant by 28, but it's just not the way it happened." Life rarely turns out the way you plan it, and egg freezing might offer an insurance policy's comfort to the handful of women who've tried it.

But most women never will, and that's the problem with the hype. It distracts from the fundamental reality that young women still have a lot of control over the big choices in their lives. Few of the professional women who can afford egg freezing would accept that going to graduate school, or getting a great job, or any of their other major life goals might not happen. Getting married and having children while you're young enough not to fret about a ticking clock can be goals, too. They were for me, which is why I took the plunge and became a 28-year-old mom this spring. In the process, I learned that having a baby while your friends are into happy hours is tough. So is trying to build a career while figuring out how to pay for babysitting. I can't claim to know my way in the world. But these issues don't go away when you're 38, or even 48, and that's the problem with putting all your eggs in a frozen basket. There's never a "best" time.

Most women seem to know this. For all the talk of professional women's dilemmas, I'm hardly the youngest mom around. The average age for first-time motherhood in the USA is 25.

The vast majority of women—who could never afford egg freezing—simply have their children when they're young and figure out the rest of their lives as they live them. It's not a bad approach. It's probably most doable if you're affluent enough to consider egg freezing in the first place. Too bad that makes for less exciting headlines, though, than putting your biological clock on ice.

13

Egg Donation Puts Donors at Risk

Jennifer Schneider

Jennifer Schneider is a physician whose daughter died of colon cancer after having donated eggs three times. Schneider, certified in internal medicine, addiction medicine, and pain management, is author of eight books and numerous articles in professional journals and has been a guest on television and radio programs.

Donating eggs to help infertile women have children is certainly admirable. However, in vitro fertilization (IVF) clinics do not adequately warn these young donors of the dangers. Because IVF clinics have an interest in promoting egg donation, they conduct little research on the long-term risks. The research that has been conducted reveals that egg donors face some risk of estrogen-related cancers. Because the public cannot count on private IVF clinics to police themselves, the government should intervene. The government in Great Britain has already done so.

The following is not an official transcript of testimony but the author's record of her testimony at the November 14, 2007, Congressional "Briefing on Human Egg Trafficking."

I'm a physician. I'm also the mother of a young woman who, like thousands of other college students at elite universities, decided to supplement her income by donating her eggs for money. And like all other egg donors, she did it without

Jennifer Schneider, "Egg Donation for IVF and Stem Cell Research: Time to Weigh the Risks to Women's Health," Testimony delivered at the Congressional Briefing on Human Egg Trafficking, November 14, 2007. Reproduced by permission of the author.

understanding that the long-term risks of this procedure are unknown. She underwent the procedure three times, and then went on with her life. Six years later she was dead of a disease that usually affects people my age, not hers—colon cancer. She had no family history of this disease, and genetic studies of her tissue subsequently showed that she was not at genetic risk of colon cancer.

Since her death I've researched what is known about the long-term risks of colon cancer in egg donors, and I'm here to tell you that hardly anything is known, because once a young woman walks out of an IVF [in vitro fertilization] clinic, she is of no interest to anyone. No one keeps track of her health. In fact, the people who benefit from egg donations—IVF clinics and researchers—have every reason to avoid follow-up of egg donors and studies of their possible long-term risks. (After Jessica's death I learned the name of her egg broker and phoned her. I told her Jessica had died of a potentially genetic disease and the broker needed to tell the recipients of Jessica's eggs about this, because their child/children will need to be tested. The broker told me that she only keeps records for a few years, and had already destroyed all records pertaining to Jessica, so that the broker no longer had information about who were the recipients. Very convenient!)

The IVF clinics make enormous sums of money from egg donation, and the researchers want to maximize the number of eggs they have. That's why, as in Great Britain, we need government intervention. I'm here to tell you why I think it is very important for Congress to mandate egg donor registries to keep track of egg donors.

An Ideal Donor

Jessica fits the classic description of an ideal egg donor: beautiful (she modeled in her teens), bright (Stanford graduate), tall (6 feet tall), athletic, talented, artistic. A short film she made at college won the first prize for best short film that year at the San Francisco Film Festival. She composed songs, played piano and guitar, and was lead singer in a rock band at college. Later she composed more classical musical.

When Jessica phoned me to tell me she was considering being an egg donor, I said, "My main concern is your safety. Is this safe?" She said, "They told me there are some risks associated with the procedure, such as bleeding or infection, and that's about it." She said, "I'm having this done at a very respected IVF clinic. I'm sure they'll take good care of me." Even though I'm a highly trained medical professional, I assumed that what she was telling me was the facts. The first time she donated her eggs, a pregnancy resulted. This made her a "proven donor," an even more desirable category. A couple of months later, the egg broker phoned her to say another couple wanted to use her, and was willing to pay twice as much. She did three egg cycles in all.

Jessica then entered a graduate school program in filmmaking, and was finishing up her master's degree when she developed abdominal pain. A work up showed advanced colon cancer, very unusual in a 29-year-old. I knew that average survival with the best treatments available was 18 months. Jessica had to drop out of school. She underwent chemotherapy, massive surgery, and radiation when she developed metastases in her bones and then her brain. She then developed metastases in her lungs and gradually lost her ability to breathe. She died at age 31.

During her almost two years of fighting her cancer, she composed a musical based on the story of "Hansel and Gretel." Her theater company planned to mount a production of this musical, and Jessica's greatest wish was to see it performed. She brought her computer with her to chemotherapy sessions and hospitalizations, and continued composing while lying in bed. But she died three weeks before her musical premiered at the New York International Fringe Festival, where it won a prize for Best Music for that year, 2003. The *New York*

Times Arts section had a lead article about Jessica and her musical. It was titled, "Premiere Draws Crowds and Tears for Absent Composer." NBC's *Today* show ran a piece about Jessica.

Her death was unexplained. When she was first diagnosed, the first thing she—and I—thought of was could it have been the large doses of hormones she received for the egg retrieval. Jessica asked her oncologist, who told her that there was no evidence supporting a role of ovarian hyperstimulation in causing colon cancer.

Egg Donors Are Commodities

But [in 2006] I ran across an article by Dr. Kamal Ahuja, a specialist in in vitro fertilization (IVF), that described a young woman who donated eggs for her infertile sister, and a few years later was diagnosed with advanced colon cancer and died. This got me thinking seriously about the possible role of ovarian stimulation in causing her colon cancer. I began doing a lot of reading, and communicating with specialists in the field. What I learned was very disturbing. Here is what I learned:

- Egg donors are commodities.

- Long-term risks of egg donation are unknown.

- IVF clinics and researchers have a serious conflict of interest.

- The government needs to intervene.

- The first baby born by in vitro fertilization (IVF) was born in 1978.

- The first IVF baby using a donated egg was born in 1984.

- In 1992 there were about 1,800 egg donor cycles.

- In 2004 there were 15,175 egg donor cycles. This exponential increase is escalating further now because of the new huge demand for eggs for stem cell research.

[A] front-page article in *Arizona Daily News* on Nov. 4, 2007, was titled "New life for sale: Human eggs focus of booming, $3B industry" and quotes,

> Caitlin K. sees it as a classic case of supply and demand. After all, one of her eggs goes to waste every month, so she might as well share it with a woman who can use it. She thinks the $8,000 she can get is a reasonable price for helping someone create a life.... Caitlin K., 24, is a bit player in a $3 billion business that is thriving on the Internet.... But as it flourished, some are warning that the freewheeling marketplace is turning the creation of human life into a commercial enterprise that cries out for consumer protection. Nowhere is this more evident than in the exploding market for human eggs, where there are few laws protecting the rights and health of donors and parents.

More from the article: "Donors are becoming more savvy.... Girls are doing it because it helps with their finances.... Would-be parents pay the fee to the egg donor themselves, in addition to the $15,000 or more that goes to the agency for insurance, and the donor's medical and legal costs." The egg broker also profits with a hefty fee. And the medical insurance purchased for the egg donor undoubtedly does not cover [later] medical costs, such as was the case with Jessica's illness.

- Egg donors are not followed up.

- They don't have their own doctors.

- The known short-term risks (ovarian hyperstimulation syndrome) are underplayed (no one told Jessica anything about this, yet young women have died).

- Long-term risks are not known.

- Egg donors sign consent forms without knowing the risks, because the risks are not known.

- Once they leave the IVF clinic they are of no interest to anyone.

Young women are unlikely to understand the huge difference between the statements "There are no known long-term risks," and "There are no long-term risks."

The Role of the Internet

The above article mentions a website called Egg Donation Inc., so I visited it. Its motto is "Where Dreams Come True." It claims to be the oldest and largest donor website in the world, with a stable of over 1,000 available egg donors. This detailed website discusses medical, legal, and psychological issues. Its emphasis is on altruism, although the reality is that the main motivator for egg donors is money. It provides testimonials from two egg donors. One says, in part, "Even since my teens I've wanted to do something that will make a difference in someone else's life." The other says, in part, "The opportunity to help someone else without wanting something back really only comes around a few times in life." The website says nothing about risks, other than in the legal section it states "medical professionals will discuss risks." . . .

I Googled "egg donation" and got 487,000 hits. Many offer payment for egg donors. Some list extremely specific characteristics they seek—particular ethnic types, religion, eye color, type of education and interests, etc.—and offer sums as high as $100,000 for the right donor.

Young women are lured by these offers. The risks are minimized. Additionally, the young women are unlikely to understand the huge difference between the statements "There are no known long-term risks," and "There are no long-term risks." Moreover, the quick money overwhelms any real attention to potential risks. Potential egg donors need their own doctor, they need an impartial person who can counsel them and who is not a part of the egg donor industry. Instead they are perceived as commodities rather than as individual human beings of value. Instead, they are counseled by employees of the egg broker and the IVF clinic, who naturally want as many women as possible to sell their eggs.

What Is Known About the Risks?

There have been no long-term studies of egg donors. There is a real need for such studies. But they will not happen until there is a mandatory egg donor registry, so that there is contact information for egg donors and they can be followed up for years.

Here's what we know so far about the relationship between hormonal stimulation and cancer:

1. Studies of infertile women who have had ovarian stimulation in order to harvest their own eggs. (They are not comparable to young egg donors—[they are] older; infertility itself is associated with increased risk of some cancers; if they get pregnant subsequently, the hormonal milieu of pregnancy may mitigate some of the effects of ovarian stimulation.) A study of over 12,000 such infertile women was published in 2005 (Altuis et al.). It found a 1.8-fold increase in the risk of uterine cancer following ovarian stimulation. The study didn't follow enough women for a long enough time, but it did find that the greater the number of years since donation, the greater the risk of breast cancer.

2. Studies of effects of female hormones in general: It is known that treatment with estrogen causes an increase in the risk of estrogen-related cancers such as breast and ovarian cancer. In the past few years, now that fewer women take hormones after menopause, there has been a decline in breast cancer. Women who have a uterus and take estrogen are at in-

creased risk of uterine cancer, which is why they are also advised to take a progesterone, which counteracts the increased risk.

Conflicts of Interest

Why are private agencies not interested in the well-being of egg donors? Because they have a lot to gain from encouraging egg donors—money from desperate infertile couples and eggs for research. IVF clinics are highly lucrative. They are the "cash cows" of university ob-gyn departments. Researchers want as many eggs as possible.

Great Britain, Canada, and Israel all have outlawed the sale of eggs.

There is now research taking place on "natural" IVF. Women don't need to be given high doses of hormones in order to produce a single egg—they do it once a month on their own. It's possible for IVF clinics to obtain a single egg from an egg donor without stimulating her ovaries, and it's clearly safer. But it's also a lot less efficient—several months of ultrasounds and egg retrieval may be necessary for a pregnancy, and certainly researchers will get fewer eggs for research. So IVF clinics and researchers are interested in getting as many eggs as possible, which involves high doses of hormones.

In 2006 the American Society of Reproductive Medicine's [ASRM's] Ethics Committee published guidelines on payments to egg donors. They suggested a "reasonable" fee of $5,000, and a maximum of $10,000. But they did not put in place any way of enforcing these guidelines, which are widely ignored. The members of ASRM are primarily physicians working in IVF clinics, the same clinics who want to attract as many donors as possible, by offering them increasingly large fees.

The Government Needs to Intervene

Private agencies and researchers can't be expected to police themselves. This reality has been recognized in other countries. Great Britain, Canada, and Israel all have outlawed the sale of eggs. Eggs are similar to other organs, and the sale of organs is outlawed in the U.S. The sale of organs is outlawed because otherwise the financial incentives may outweigh consideration of the donor's best interest. The U.S., on the other hand, seems to consider egg donation in the same category as sperm donation rather than subject to existing laws regarding organ donation. Clearly, sperm donation does not involve risks, unlike egg donation.

There is urgent need for proper oversight and medical care of egg donors. There are two patients—the infertile woman and the egg donor. It's time that the egg donor ceases to be the forgotten member of the team. This country needs a comprehensive egg donor registry, which will enable research on the long-term effects of egg donation.

Seeking Egg Donors in Developing Nations Exploits Poor Women

Antony Barnett and Helena Smith

Antony Barnett is a British investigative journalist who writes for the Guardian *and its sister paper, the* Observer. *Helena Smith is the* Guardian's *correspondent in Greece, Turkey, and Cyprus.*

One of the shameful consequences of the growth of assisted reproduction is that in vitro fertilization clinics often exploit poor women at the expense of their physical and mental health. In Eastern Europe and Cyprus, for example, poor women are donating their eggs so that they can make ends meet. Unfortunately, women who donate eggs sometimes suffer serious side effects that can prove fatal. Egg donation also can have psychological effects. Some of these women feel like they have sold part of their body, and others wonder about their unknown children. Wealthy women should not be able to have children at the expense of women struggling to survive.

Svetlana has a big family secret: she sold her eggs for US dollars. Svetlana did not tell her husband what she was doing because she knew he would be furious. Nor did she tell her mother or her two young children. Every day after lunch this 27-year-old unemployed cook would sneak out of her cramped, Soviet-era tower block on the outskirts of the Ukrainian capital, Kiev, to go for hormone injections that would stimulate her ovaries into producing dozens of eggs. Each one of these had the potential of becoming a relative that her family would never know about.

Donating eggs ... can be a lengthy, painful and potentially dangerous procedure involving the injection of a powerful drug known as follicle stimulating hormone.

Desperate for money after the birth of her second child, Svetlana had applied for work in the canteen of one of Kiev's growing number of fertility clinics that charge infertile women from Britain thousands of pounds for help in getting them pregnant. Svetlana didn't get the job, but was told that if she needed cash she could sell her eggs. She was told that the process was straightforward and that she would be given $300— more if she was a good donor and produced lots of eggs.

For Svetlana, like a growing number of Eastern European women, it was too good an opportunity to pass up. Since the birth of her second child she had been surviving on less than $15 a month. She turned out to be an excellent donor. By the time of her fifth donation, her ovaries, stimulated by the injection of a hormone, produced a batch of 40 healthy eggs. This is four times more eggs than a woman undergoing IVF would produce.

The medical staff gave Svetlana an extra $200 as a reward. For the clinic, Svetlana was a cash cow, a woman whose eggs could be sold for profit. Older women from Britain, the US and other Western countries whose ovaries can no longer produce healthy eggs are happy to pay more than £3,000 for donor eggs that could be fertilised into an embryo. The hope is that, once implanted back into the woman, they will conceive the 'miracle' baby that has so far eluded them.

A Potentially Dangerous Procedure

Yet what Svetlana didn't know is that donating eggs is not a straightforward matter like donating sperm. It can be a lengthy, painful and potentially dangerous procedure involving the injection of a powerful drug known as follicle stimulating hormone, or FSH. Medical experts believe 1 per cent of women undergoing this can suffer serious side-effects known as ovarian hyper-stimulation syndrome (OHSS) that in extreme cases can prove fatal.

One leading British fertility expert, Adam Balen, Professor of Reproductive Medicine at Leeds General Hospital, believes the fact that Svetlana produced 40 eggs is evidence that she was being hyper-stimulated by the clinic and her health was being put at risk. At no time did the medical staff at the Kiev clinic explain anything to Svetlana or give her any counselling on the psychological impact of donating eggs. Svetlana found out she was being injected with hormones only when, on the fourth time, she had to be put on a drip. She was told the injections were to 'clean her blood'. Other complications included missing her period for two months and stomach pains.

All the [Ukrainian] donors ... have one thing in common: they all sold their eggs for the money, all have regrets about what they did, and none would do it again.

A year after her last donation, Svetlana meets at a secret location to tell her story. She is scared of being seen speaking to a journalist near her home. She has had no lasting physical problems, but is affected psychologically. 'I feel like I sold part of my body,' she explains. What did she think about the possibility that she may have children in London and her son may have a half-brother? 'They will be two now, but I try not to think about it. Hopefully they don't look like me. My two children look like their father, so I hope that is the case.'

She has kept her egg donation a secret from most people: 'I don't want anybody to know; for me it's unpleasant that I have sold a part of myself. That I have sold myself for money. Many people wouldn't understand it.'

A Global Trade

An investigation by the *Observer* has revealed a burgeoning global trade in women's eggs where infertile British women who cannot find a donor in the UK will pay thousands of pounds for the chance of finding one overseas.

Svetlana is typical of dozens of young Ukrainian women desperate for cash having to sell their eggs to make ends meet. While most sell them in Kiev, others are sent by Ukrainian clinics to Cyprus or even Belize. Their Caucasian appearance is turning young East European women into a source for one of the continent's most prized commodities: human eggs.

It is a trade conducted in the utmost secrecy, with donors' identity strictly protected. Yet the *Observer* tracked down several other egg donors in Kiev who, like Svetlana, have sold eggs to clinics that helped British women to conceive. Some of the girls are unemployed or working in low-paid menial jobs, others are former graduates now earning good salaries; some are blonde, while others are brown-haired with dark eyes. But all the donors we spoke to have one thing in common: they all sold their eggs for the money, all have regrets about what they did, and none would do it again.

'We only did it for the money,' says Erena, who donated four times and knows more than 20 donors who gave eggs to one of the city's clinics. She claims that one young girl she knew donated nearly 20 times and none of the girls was given any psychological counselling. She said they were given more money the more eggs they produced.

Erena recalls that once she was injected with five ampoules of FSH. Each capsule contained 75 units of the hormone, so she received 375 units. According to Balen, this is a potentially dangerous amount that could spark OHSS. 'For a young woman with healthy ovaries, I would use no more than 150 units of FSH or you run the risk of OHSS. Although serious complications are rare, they can be extremely serious and even fatal.' Balen was particularly concerned at the sliding scale of fees paid which would encourage donors to accept more hormones in the hope of more money. 'It sounds more like egg farming to me than egg donation,' he said. Erena says she felt she was treated like a 'milking cow'.

In today's global market, a healthy human egg from a young white European woman is more valuable than gold. . . .

Should the rights of a British woman desperate for a family supersede the rights of a poor East European forced to sell her eggs for cash?

A Hidden Nightmare

A trade that can fulfil the dream of a British couple can be a hidden nightmare for the donor. While there is no denying the joy of an infertile woman who has been able to have a baby using an overseas donor, there can be an unsavoury underside to the process where poor young women are exploited, injected with potentially dangerous hormones and treated like 'battery hens' being farmed for their eggs. These are women who are the secret mothers of British children, parents who will never know their genetic children. It is what the chair of the HFEA [Human Fertilisation and Embryology Authority], Suzi Leather, has called a 'profoundly exploitative and unethical trade'.

Should the rights of a British woman desperate for a family supersede the rights of a poor East European forced to sell her eggs for cash? If the foreign clinics can assure that donors are not exploited, is there a problem? Are the strict British regulations helping to create an unsavoury market in human eggs?

Leather said: 'The market in babymaking is now global and these problems have to be tackled internationally. This compelling testimony shows the nasty underside of a global market in babymaking and should act as a wake-up call.'

Near the little fishing village of Sygi on Cyprus sits an unassuming stone building surrounded by palm trees and with its own private beach. In [2005] hundreds of women referred by fertility doctors in Britain have checked in here. This is the Petra Health Clinic, an offshoot of the Reproductive Genetics Institute in Chicago. The *Observer* has been told that it was its offices in Kiev that paid Ukrainian girls $500 to fly to this clinic and donate eggs. In its waiting room, couples are usually met by Galina Ivanovina, the clinic's resident Russian director.

Treatment for multi-embryo implants involving an egg donor from the clinic costs $5,000. Ivanovina claims they do not pay donors. 'We put them up in flats and give them a free holiday, but now, it seems, they feel they can pay for their own. If you wish you can pay them too.' Ivanovina says the waiting list is only two months' long, which gives clients time to think about the perfect 'donor match'.

'Do you want a baby that looks like you, a little bit Slavic?' she asks an undercover *Observer* reporter who inquired about the possibility of donor egg and donor sperm. On request she produces an itemised description of a woman who donated eggs at the clinic, 'Nationality, Russian; height, 1.69m; weight, 55 kilos; blood type, ABIV+; hair colour, brown; eye colour, brown; education, higher technical college; occupation, engineer.'

Ivanovina says: 'This would be a typical donor. All of our donors are from Eastern Europe, Russia, Ukraine.'

Dr Vasillis Thanos, the Israeli-trained gynaecologist who oversees embryo transfers at the clinic, says female donors get 'free of charge' gynaecological treatment throughout their lives. 'These ladies are very well selected; they approach doctors who give them all the information about the whole procedure. They do it for altruistic reasons. So far, not one of these ladies has ever had any somatic or psychological problems,' he insists. 'They are absolutely from good families; they have children. They are checked in Russia for genetic diseases and psychiatric diseases.'

According to the information obtained by the *Observer* under FOI [Freedom of Information act] one British clinic that has been sending several couples to Cyprus is the fertility centre at the private Cromwell Hospital, the exclusive private hospital in Central London. Dr Kamal Ahuja, who runs it, says that the Petra Clinic operates to the highest international standards and has an impressive donor-screening programme.

Some [Russian donors] viewed egg donation as their main source of income, going through the process of being injected with hormones at least five times a year.

A Source of Needed Income

An estimated 30,000 immigrants from the former Soviet Union live in Cyprus, even if only half are legally registered with the authorities. Local Russian-language newspapers often place advertisements seeking 'young healthy girls for egg donation'. Women from the community tracked down by the *Observer* suggested that 'one in four' of their peers had, at some point in their twenties, donated eggs. Women from Russia and Ukraine fly in just to donate eggs. Most desperately needed the money for rent and utility bills.

Larissa Kovoritsa, a nurse who mediates between Russian donors and a fertility clinic in Nicosia, told the *Observer* that some women viewed egg donation as their main source of income, going through the process of being injected with hormones at least five times a year. The going rate, she said, was 350 Cyprus pounds (£420) for a cycle in which a woman produced 12 eggs; £500 Cyprus if she produced more. 'For them it's like giving blood, you give and then you forget,' said Tatjana, a 28-year-old tour representative who is from Minsk, Belarus. 'They just give their eggs and get the money, it's a pure transaction.'

Although Tatjana says she has never been a donor herself, she came close to being one eight years ago when she moved to the island and knows many girls who have been donors. Two things stopped her: fear of side-effects and 'it just felt very strange to think that there would be a piece of me, some little Tatjana, out there in the world'.

Meeting at a secret location for fear her Greek Cypriot husband might discover the nature of our discussion, she said many women came to Cyprus from the states of 'new Europe'—Poland, Lithuania, Latvia, Estonia. 'They work the cabarets, they'll sleep with men, they'll sell their eggs, and then they go back again.'

Two of her four friends spoke to the *Observer* on a confidential basis. They admitted they had never been pregnant before, in contravention of UK regulations. 'I was never told I would have to go through psychological tests,' said 33-year-old Yelena from Moscow, who was a donor in her mid-twenties. 'The only paper I was made to sign was one saying I gave up all my rights to the child, which was OK because now I have two of my own and really don't want to think about the past. That was then, when I was hungry and desperate.' But Tatjana agreed that the fees were still 'very attractive. . . . In Russia you can live off $1,000 for an entire year.'

And would there be no curiosity about the child? 'You know, you can play with your own psychology,' she says. 'In Russia when they execute somebody there is always one soldier who doesn't have a bullet, so in the end nobody is really sure who shot the man. It's a bit like that here. Not all embryo [implants] are successful. In the end, you can never be guaranteed that it was your egg that was the one that was used.'

Organizations to Contact

The editors have compiled the following list of organizations concerned with the issues debated in this book. The descriptions are derived from materials provided by the organizations. All have publications or information available for interested readers. The list was compiled on the date of publication of the present volume; the information provided here may change. Be aware that many organizations take several weeks or longer to respond to inquiries, so allow as much time as possible.

American Medical Association (AMA)
515 N. State St., Chicago, IL   60610
(312) 464-5000
Web site: www.ama-assn.org

AMA is the largest professional association for medical doctors. It helps set standards for medical education and practices, and it is a powerful lobby in Washington for physicians' interests. The association publishes specific journals for many medical fields and the AMA's weekly journal *JAMA*. It also publishes a magazine of current issues important to physicians, the bimonthly *AMA Voice*, past issues of which are available on its Web site. Also on its Web site, the AMA publishes fact sheets that explain the reasoning behind its code of medical ethics concerning reproductive technology, including "Ethical Conduct in Assisted Reproductive Technology" and "Frozen Pre-Embryos."

American Public Health Association (APHA)
800 I St. NW, Washington, DC   20001-3710
(202) 777-APHA • fax: (202) 777-2534
e-mail: comments@apha.org
Web site: www.apha.org

Founded in 1872, the American Public Health Association consists of more than fifty thousand individuals and organizations that aim to improve public health. Its members represent over fifty public health occupations, including researchers, practitioners, administrators, teachers, and other health care workers. APHA publishes the monthly newspaper *The Nation's Health* and the *American Journal of Public Health*, recent issues of which are available on its Web site. Also on its Web site are recent reports of its Emerging Reproductive Technologies Task Force. The task force currently focuses on assisted reproductive technologies, genetic screening, and the use of women's eggs for stem cell research.

American Society for Reproductive Medicine (ASRM)
1209 Montgomery Highway, Birmingham, AL   35216-2809
(205) 978-5000 • fax: (205) 978-5005
e-mail: asrm@asrm.org
Web site: www.asrm.org

Founded by a small group of fertility experts, ASRM sets standards in the field of reproductive medicine. The society helps develop new medical approaches, forms key legislation, and fights for reproductive rights. It publishes the journal *Fertility and Sterility* and two newsletters, *ASRM News* and *Menopausal Medicine*. The society publishes ethical guidelines, minimum standards, committee opinions, and technical and educational bulletins. For patients, the ASRM publishes booklets and fact sheets designed to help patients understand the complexities of reproductive disorders and their treatment. Many of these publications are available on the organization's Web site.

Biotechnology Industry Organization (BIO)
1201 Maryland Ave. SW, Suite 900, Washington, DC   20024
(202) 962-9200 • fax: (202) 488-9601
e-mail: info@bio.org
Web site: www.bio.org

BIO represents biotechnology companies, academic institutions, state biotechnology centers, and related organizations that support the use of biotechnology in improving health care, agriculture, efforts to clean up the environment, and other fields. BIO works to educate the public about biotechnology and responds to concerns about the safety of genetic engineering and reproductive technologies. It publishes *Bioethics: Facing the Future Responsibly* and an introductory guide to biotechnology, which are available on the organization's Web site.

Center for Bioethics and Human Dignity (CBHD)

2065 Half Day Road, Bannockburn, IL   60015
(847) 317-8180 • fax: (847) 317-8101
e-mail: info@cbhd.org
Web site: www.cbhd.org

CBHD is an international education center, the purpose of which is to bring Christian perspectives to bear on contemporary bioethical challenges facing society. Its publications address genetic technologies as well as other topics such as euthanasia and abortion. It publishes the book *Cutting-Edge Bioethics* and the audio CD *The Challenges and Opportunities of Genetic Intervention*. The articles "Biotechnology's Brave New World," "Infertility Technology Run Amok: Women Not Meant to Carry 'Litters' of Children," and "Sex and Desire: The Role of Parental Aspiration in Sex Selection" are available on the organization's Web site.

Centers for Disease Control and Prevention (CDC)

1600 Clifton Road, Atlanta, GA   30333
(404) 639-3534
Web site: www.cdc.gov/ART

The goal of the CDC is to protect health and promote quality of life through the prevention and control of disease, injury, and disability. It supports programs that reduce the health and economic consequences of the leading causes of death and disability. The Assisted Reproductive Technology (ART) section of the CDC Web site publishes annual reports regarding the success rate of ART and related resources, including a bibliography of articles related to ART.

Council for Responsible Genetics (CRG)
5 Upland Road, Suite 3, Cambridge, MA   02140
(617) 868-0870 • fax: (617) 491-5344
e-mail: crg@gene-watch.org
Web site: www.councilforresponsiblegenetics.org

CRG is a national nonprofit organization of scientists, public health advocates, and others who promote a comprehensive public interest agenda for biotechnology. Its members work to raise public awareness about genetic issues, including genetic discrimination. CRG publishes *GeneWatch* magazine, providing access to current and archived articles on its Web site. The council also publishes a Genetic Bill of Rights to encourage dialogue on the fundamental values that the council believes have been put at risk by new applications of genetics.

The Hastings Center
21 Malcolm Gordon Road, Garrison, NY   10524-5555
(845) 424-4040 • fax: (845) 424-4545
e-mail: mail@thehastingscenter.org
Web site: www.thehastingscenter.org

The Hastings Center is an independent research institute that explores the medical, ethical, and social ramifications of biomedical advances. The center publishes books, including *Reprogenetics*, the bimonthly *Hastings Center Report,* and the bimonthly newsletter *IRB: Ethics and Human Research.* Articles and commentary available on its Web site include "Authenticity and Ambivalence: Toward Understanding the Enhancement Debate" and "Are Parents Driven to Design Their Babies?"

National Institute of Child Health and Human Development (NICHD)
31 Center Drive, Building 31, Room 2A32, MSC 2425
Bethesda, MD   20892-2425
(301) 402-0911 • fax: (301) 402-2218

e-mail: NICHDInformationResourceCenter@mail.nih.gov
Web site: www.nichd.nih.gov

The NICHD, part of the National Institutes of Health, conducts and supports research on topics related to the health of children, adults, and families, including reducing infant deaths, improving the health of women, men, and families, and understanding reproductive health and fertility. Relevant articles on reproductive technologies are available on its Web site.

National Women's Health Information Center (NWHIC)
8270 Willow Oaks Corporate Drive, Fairfax, VA   22031
(800) 994-9662
Web site: www.womenshealth.gov

The NWHIC is a service of the Office on Women's Health in the Department of Health and Human Services. It provides access to current and reliable information on a wide array of women's health issues. The organization publishes a monthly newsletter, *Healthy Women Today*, recent issues of which are available on its Web site as are other NWHIC resources.

President's Council on Bioethics
1425 New York Ave. NW, Suite C100
Washington, DC   20005
(202) 296-4669
e-mail: info@bioethics.gov
Web site: www.bioethics.gov

When the National Bioethics Advisory Commission's charter expired in October 2001, President George W. Bush established the President's Council on Bioethics. The group works to protect the rights and welfare of human research subjects and to govern the management and use of genetic information. On its Web site, the Council provides access to its reports "Reproduction and Responsibility: The Regulation of New Biotechnologies" and "Beyond Therapy: Biotechnology and the Pursuit of Happiness."

Resolve: The National Infertility Association
1760 Old Meadow Road, Suite 500, McLean, VA 22102
(703) 556-7172 • fax: (703) 506-3266
Web site: www.resolve.org

Resolve is a nonprofit, nationwide network dedicated to providing support, promoting reproductive health, and ensuring equal access to all family-building options for men and women experiencing infertility or other reproductive disorders. Its Web site provides fact sheets on fertility issues and reproductive technologies. Its online network, Resolve 2.0, provides patients with an online support community and connects patients and professionals. It also provides access to a resource library and the latest infertility-related blogs, news, and videos.

Stanford University Center for Biomedical Ethics (SCBE)
701 Welch Road, Building A, Suite 1105
Palo Alto, CA 94304
(650) 723-5760 • fax: (650) 725-6131
e-mail: SCBE-info@med.stanford.edu
Web site: http://scbe.stanford.edu

SCBE engages in interdisciplinary research on moral questions arising from the complex relationships among medicine, science, and society. The center is committed to exploring and promoting compassionate approaches to the practice of medicine in a climate of socioeconomic and technological change. SCBE publishes the newsletter *Stanford Bioethics*, recent issues of which are available on its Web site.

World Future Society
7910 Woodmont Ave., Suite 450, Bethesda, MD 20814
(301) 656-8274 • fax: (301) 951-0394
e-mail: info@wfs.org
Web site: www.wfs.org

The society serves as a national clearinghouse for ideas and information about the future, including forecasts, recommendations, and alternative scenarios. These ideas help people to

anticipate what may happen in coming years and to distinguish between possible, probable, and desired futures. The society publishes the bimonthly *Futurist* magazine and *Futures
Research Quarterly*. On its Web site the society publishes lists
of recommended books on issues concerning humanity's future, including reproductive technologies.

Bibliography

Books

Gautam Allahbadia — *The Art and Science of Assisted Reproductive Techniques*. New York: Taylor and Francis, 2004.

Ivo Brosens — *The Challenge of Reproductive Medicine at Catholic Universities; Time to Leave the Catacombs*. Dudley, MA: Peeters, 2006.

Lorraine Culley, Nicky Hudson, and Floor van Rooij, eds. — *Marginalized Reproduction: Ethnicity, Infertility, and Reproductive Technologies*. London: Earthscan, 2009.

Tommaso Falcone — *Overcoming Infertility*. Cleveland, OH: Cleveland Clinic Press, 2006.

David K. Gardner — *In Vitro Fertilization: A Practical Approach*. New York: Informa Healthcare, 2007.

Joan Haran, et al. — *Human Cloning in the Media: From Science Fiction to Science Practice*. New York: Routledge, 2008.

John Harris — *On Cloning*. New York: Routledge, 2004.

Kirsty Horsey and Hazel Biggs — *Human Fertilisation and Embryology: Reproducing Regulation*. London: Routledge-Cavendish, 2007.

Joseph H. Howell and William F. Sale — *Life Choices: A Hastings Center Introduction to Bioethics*. Washington, DC: Georgetown University Press, 2000.

Richard T. Hull, ed. — *Ethical Issues in the New Reproductive Technologies*. Amherst, NY: Prometheus, 2005.

Kerry Lynn Macintosh — *Illegal Beings: Human Clones and the Law*. New York: Cambridge University Press, 2005.

Ramez Naam — *More Than Human: Embracing the Promise of Biological Enhancement*. New York, Broadway Books, 2005.

Peggy Orenstein — *Waiting for Daisy: A Tale of Two Continents, Three Religions, Five Infertility Doctors, an Oscar, an Atomic Bomb, a Romantic Night, and One Woman's Quest to Become a Mother*. New York: Bloomsbury, 2007.

Christopher Thomas Scott — *Stem Cell Now: From the Experiment That Shook the World to the New Politics of Life*. New York: Pi Press, 2006.

Debora L. Spar — *The Baby Business: How Money, Science, and Politics Drive the Commerce of Conception*. Boston: Harvard Business School Press, 2006.

Alastair G. Sutcliffe, ed. — *Health and Welfare of ART Children*. London: Informa Healthcare, 2006.

Alan O. Trounson and David K. Gardner, eds.   *Handbook of In Vitro Fertilization.* Boca Raton, FL: CRC Press, 2000.

Ian Wilmut   *After Dolly: The Uses and Misuses of Human Cloning.* New York: Norton, 2006.

Periodicals

Claudia Anderson   "The Parent Hood: How Technology and Social Progress Are Turning Procreation into Self-Actualization," *Weekly Standard,* December 1, 2006.

Francoise Baylis, Jeff Nisker, and Susan Sherwin   "Nothing Extreme About Protecting Fresh Embryos," *Globe and Mail* (Toronto), January 16, 2007.

Greg Bear   "Is Artificial Life Moving Any Closer?" *Nature,* November 2007.

Tom Carney   "Status of Frozen Embryos Sparks Moral Debate," *National Catholic Reporter,* March 3, 2006.

Alan H. DeCherney   "How Safe Is Safe Enough? Obligations to the Children of Reproductive Technology," *New England Journal of Medicine,* March 31, 2005.

Cheryl Erwin   "Utopian Dreams and Harsh Realities: Who Is in Control of Assisted Reproductive Technologies in a High-Tech World?" *Journal of Gender, Race, and Justice,* Spring 2006.

Mark Henderson "Career Women Warned Against Egg Freezing," *Times Online*, October 17, 2007.

Francis Kane "Begotten, Not Made: The Dangers of Reproductive Technology," *Commonweal*, February 15, 2008.

Bartha M. Knoppers and Rosario M. Isasi "Regulatory Approaches to Reproductive Genetic Testing," *Human Reproduction*, December 1, 2004.

Timothy Krahn "Where Are We Going with Preimplantation Genetic Diagnosis?" *Canadian Medical Association Journal*, 2007.

Cheryl Miller "Who's Your Daddy? Children of Sperm Donors Are Seeking More Information About Their Once-Anonymous Fathers, Sometimes at the Risk of the Fertility Industry Itself," *Reason*, February 1, 2009.

Penni Mitchell "Keep Your Hands Off Our Ovaries!" *Herizons*, Fall 2006.

Timothy F. Murphy and Gladys B. White "Dead Sperm Donors or World Hunger: Are Bioethicists Studying the Right Stuff?" *Hasting Center Report*, March/April 2005.

New Scientist "Beyond IVF: Should Parents Be Free to Decide What Is Acceptable?" October 21, 2006.

Peggy Orenstein   "Your Gamete, Myself," *New York Times*, July 15, 2007.

John Patten   "Not Even Science Fiction Foresaw the End of Fathers," *Spectator*, May 3, 2008.

Shari Roan   "The Embryo Dilemma: In Support of Science," *Los Angeles Times*, October 6, 2008.

Bonnie Miller Rubin   "Egg Donation Has Become a Booming Business for Donors, Recruiters," *Chicago Tribune*, March 8, 2007.

William Saletan   "Cut-Off Genes: Our Gentle Descent Toward Eugenics," *Slate*, May 19, 2006.

William Saletan   "Where Do Babies Come From?" *Washington Post*, September 17, 2006.

Preeti Shekar   "Reproductive Racism: Gender Selection Technologies Target Asian Communities," *Colorlines*, September/October 2007.

Emily Singer   "Choosing Babies," *Technology Review*, March 1, 2007.

Margaret Somerville   "The Ethical Minefield of Multiple Births," *Vancouver Sun* (Australia), December 27, 2008.

Debora Spar   "The Egg Trade—Making Sense of the Market for Human Oocytes," *New England Journal of Medicine*, March 29, 2007.

John Thavis "Vatican Document Warns Certain New Research Violates Moral Principles," *Catholic Spirit*, December 12, 2008.

Rebecca Tuhus-Dubrow "ART in America," *Nation*, November 26, 2007.

Valerie Ulene "Babies, the Easy Way? Used to Treat Infertility, Reproductive Technology Should Not Be Entered Into Lightly; It Could Pose Risks to the Unborn Child," *Los Angeles Times*, August 11, 2008.

Barbara Dafoe Whitehead "Answered Prayers," *Commonweal*, October 20, 2006.

Index

A

Abortion, 36, 37, 84, 85
Adoption, 40, 51
Afraid of Human Cloning? (Pence), 12
Ahuja, Kamal, 99, 111
AID (artificial insemination–donor sperm), 18
Albert Einstein College of Medicine, 69
American College of Obstetricians and Gynecologists (ACOG), 70, 74
American Society of Reproductive Medicine (ASRM), 8, 25, 69, 86, 87, 94, 103
Andrews, Eve, 44
Anemia, 8
Arab/Muslim parents, 71, 73
Arendt, Hannah, 22
Arizona Daily News, 100
ART. *See* Assisted reproductive technology (ART)
Artificial eggs, 26, 50
Artificial insemination, 43
Artificial insemination–donor sperm (AID), 18
Artificial sperm, 26, 50
Asch, Ricardo, 14
Asian-Indian parents, 71, 73, 78–79
Assisted reproductive technology (ART), 18, 20, 25, 29, 34–36
Athletic prowess, 56, 58–59
Australia, 43, 80

B

Babies by Design: The Ethics of Genetic Choice (Green), 56, 58–59
Bailey, Ronald, 33–38
Baird, Eisenstadt v., 37
Balen, Adam, 107, 108–109
Barad, David H., 69–75
Barnett, Antony, 105–112
Belarus, 112
Belize, 108
Bell, Buck v., 36, 61
Beltsos, Angeline, 9
Beyond Bioethics: A Proposal for Modernizing the Regulation of Human Biotechnologies (Furger and Fukuyama), 24, 28, 34
Bioethics, 12
Biology
    importance to child, 44–46, 51
    importance to parents, 40–41
    ooplasm transfers, 25, 34, 49–50
Birth control, 36–37, 85
Birth defects, 8, 13
Blindness, 8
Blood clots, 8
Brown, Louise, 12–13, 15
Buck v. Bell, 36, 61
Bush, George W., 84

C

California, 10, 44, 82
Callahan, Sidney, 51
Canada, 80, 103, 104

Cancer, 94, 97–99, 102–103

Caucasian parents, 71, 74

Center for Genetics and Society, 78

Center for Human Reproduction, 69

Center for Marriage and Families, 39

Centers for Disease Control and Prevention, 13, 24

Cerebral palsy, 8

Chakravarty, Atashi, 79

Child abuse, 46

Children. *See* Customized children; Donor-conceived children; Sex selection

Children's rights, 40–41

China, 78–79

Chinese parents, 71, 73, 78–79

City of God (St. Augustine), 23

Cloning

books about, 12

government regulation and, 30, 35, 48

individuality and, 19

psychological harm and, 52

replacement children and, 19

reproductive control and, 19–20

reproductive technology and, 12

responsibility for mistakes in, 17

Time magazine and, 18

Cognitive traits, 27, 56

Colon cancer, 97–99

Competitive advantage, 58–59, 62–65

Comstock Laws, 36

Conceptus, 83

Connecticut, 36

Consent

donor-conceived children and, 29, 43

egg donation and, 101–102

Contraception, 36–37, 85

Cost of reproductive technologies

in vitro fertilization (IVF) and, 9, 13, 110

inequality issues and, 55, 59

taxpayers and, 10

Counseling, 81, 90, 107, 108

Crime, 46

Cromwell Hospital, 111

Customized children

athletic prowess and, 56, 58–59

competitive advantage and, 58–59, 62–65

control over nature and, 63

eugenics and, 61–62

germline genetic modification, 27, 30, 35, 56–57

giftedness and, 63–64, 67–68

hubris of parents and, 64–65

hyperparenting and, 65–66

privatized eugenics and, 62

sex selection, 20, 26, 27, 30

socioeconomic class and, 62

solidarity and, 67–68

technological developments and, 27

Cyprus, 108, 110, 111, 112

Cytoplasm, 25

D

Dahl, E., 72, 75

Deafness, 64

Dear Abby, 45

Designer children. *See* Customized children

Developmental issues, 8

Diabetes, 90

Dion, Celine, 89

Disease inheritance
 germline genetic modification
  and, 30, 35, 56–57
 hemophilia, 21
 preimplantation genetic diagnosis (PGD) and, 55–56,
  57–58

Divorce, 17, 46

Domestic violence, 79

Donation of eggs, 96–104

Donation of sperm, 16, 20, 42–44,
 48–49, 107

Donation of unused embryos, 81,
 86–88

Donor-conceived children
 consent and, 29, 43
 genetic heritage and, 43
 identity issues, 42–45, 51
 importance of biology and,
  44–46
 legality of parentage and,
  48–49
 personal stories, 43–45
 See also Parenthood

Doping, 56, 58–59

Down syndrome, 66–68

E

Education, 46

Egg donation
 cancer and, 96–100, 102–103
 costs, 111–112
 exploitation of poor women
  and, 105–112
 government regulation and,
  97, 106
 income source for donors, 111
 medical treatment for donors,
  110–111
 ovarian stimulation and, 99–
  103, 106–109
 psychological effects of donating eggs, 105–108, 111
 research on aftereffects, 96, 97,
  102–103
 risks, 96–104
 statistics, 43, 99–100
 stem cell research and, 100
 trade in eggs, 103–104

Egg Donation Inc., 101

Egg donor registries, 97

Eggs
 artificial eggs, 26
 donation, 43, 96–104
 stem cell creation of eggs, 26,
  34, 50
 trade in human eggs, 26, 35,
  37, 103–104, 108–109
 See also Donor-conceived children

Eisenstadt v. Baird, 37

Elspas, Janis, 81–82, 85, 91

Embryo rights, 84

Embryos
 average number in storage, 89
 counseling and, 81, 90
 disposal of unused embryos,
  81–91
 divorce and, 17
 donation of unused embryos,
  81, 86–88
 expiration date for frozen embryos, 90–91
 motherhood delay and, 92–95
 oocyte preservation, 93
 patenting embryos, 35
 research using, 14–15, 81, 83,
  87, 88
 sale, 34, 35

See also In vitro fertilization (IVF)
Environmental Protection Agency, 31
Estonia, 112
Estrogen, 102–103
Ethics
  child's best interest and, 58
  eugenics and, 61
  gene manipulation and, 58–59, 62–63
  giftedness and, 63–64
  government regulation and, 28–30, 35
  reproductive technologies and, 14, 20–21
  sex selection and, 69–80
Ethics Committee of American College of Obstetricians and Gynecologists (ACOG), 70, 74
Ethics Committee of the American Society for Reproductive Medicine (ASRM), 69, 103
Eugenics, 36, 38, 61–62
Everything Conceivable (Mundy), 81
Extend Fertility, 93

F

Family balancing, 70–72, 74, 78
Federal Drug Administration, 30
Female infanticide, 76, 77
Fertility and Sterility (journal), 86
Fertility clinics, 24–25, 77–79, 81, 106
Fertility drugs, 7, 83
Fertility Institutes (Los Angeles), 77–79
Fetal rights laws, 84
Feticide, 76, 77

Flesh of My Flesh: The Ethics of Human Cloning (Pence), 12
Follicle stimulating hormone (FSH), 107–109
Food and Drug Administration, 35
Fraud, 14
Frozen embryos, 17, 81–91, 90–91
Fukuyama, Francis, 24–38, 47–50, 53
Furger, Franco, 24–32, 34, 47–50, 53
Futurist (magazine), 55

G

Gays and lesbians, 26, 43
Gender selection. See Sex-selection technology
Gendercide, 76
Gene doping, 56, 58–59
Genesis, 21, 23
Genetic enhancement, 56
Genetic heritage, 43, 53–54
Genetics and IVF Institute, 76, 78, 79
Genetics and Public Policy Center, 27
Genocide, 61
Germline genetic modification, 27, 30, 35, 48, 56–57
Gibbs, Nancy, 7, 10
Giftedness, 63–64, 67–68
Gleicher, Norbert, 69–75
Government regulation
  contraception regulations, 36–37
  egg donation, 97, 104
  ethics and, 28–30, 35
  eugenics laws, 36

in vitro fertilization and,
50–51
need for, 28–30, 104
psychological effects of regulation, 52–53
recommendations for, 30–32
reproductive technologies and,
9, 26–27
research regulation, 15
sex selection and, 35, 37
sterilization, 36
Great Britain. *See* United Kingdom
Grech, Narelle, 43–44
Greed, 14
Green, Ronald M., 10, 56
Greenawalt, Lindsay, 44
Grindhopping: Build a Rewarding Career Without Paying Your Dues (Vanderkam), 92
Griswold, Megan, 92–93
Griswold v. Connecticut, 37
Grompe, Markus, 57
Guardian (newspaper), 105

H

Hastings Center, 47
Heart problems, 8, 59
Hemophilia, 21
Hispanic parents, 71, 74
Hitler, Adolf, 61
Holly Farms, 17
Holmes, Oliver Wendell, 61
Hormonal stimulation, 99–103,
106, 108–109
House of Commons Science and Technology Committee, 71
How to Build a Better Human: An Ethical Blueprint (Pence), 12
Hubris of parents, 64–65

Human–animal chimeras and hybrids, 29, 30, 35, 48
Human Fertilisation and Emryology Authority (HFEA) of Great Britain, 34, 36, 37, 58, 109–110
Hyperparenting, 65–66
Hypertension, 8

I

ICSI (intracytoplasmic sperm injection), 18
Identity, 42–45, 51
Illegal Beings: Human Clones and the Law (Macintosh), 52
In vitro fertilization (IVF)
costs, 12, 13, 110
exploitation of poor women and, 105–112
fears about, 12–13
government regulation and,
50–51
insurance coverage and, 13, 15
multiple births and, 7, 8,
81–82
process, 7, 94
regulation, 34
sex selection and, 70, 77
Suleman and, 7
See also Embryos
India, 78–79
Indian parents, 71, 73, 78–79
Indiana, 36
Individuality, 19, 22–23
Infant mortality, 46
Informed consent, 29, 43
Institute for American values, 39
Institute of Public Affairs and Civic Engagement, 16
Insurance coverage, 12, 13
Intelligence, 27, 56

Interest groups, 31
International Federation of Gynecology and Obstetrics, 70
International Human Genome Project, 55
Internet, 101–102
Interracial couples, 37, 53
Intracytoplasmic sperm injection (ICSI), 18
Israel, 103, 104
Ivanovina, Galina, 110
IVF. *See* In vitro fertilization (IVF)

J

Jacobson, Cecil, 14
Jain, T., 71
Japan, 45
Jaundice, 8
Jeremiahs, 12
Jesudason, Sujatha, 78
Johns Hopkins University, 24, 33, 57
Johnston, Josephine, 47–54
Judaism, 91
Juvenile diabetes, 90

K

Kamrava, Michael, 8
Kane, Francis, 16–23
Kass, Leon, 13, 57
Klock, Susan, 86
Kornberg, Warren, 14
Kovoritsa, Larissa, 111

L

Latvia, 112
Leather, Suzi, 109
Leeds General Hospital, 107

Lesbians and gays, 26, 43
Libertarians, 26–27
Life's beginnings, 84–85
Lithuania, 112
Loving v. Virginia, 37
Lung problems, 8

M

Macintosh, Kerry Lynn, 52
Magnus, David C., 9
Marquardt, Elizabeth, 39–46
Marriage, 46
Massachusetts, 37, 93
May, William, 22, 64
McCaughey, Bobbi, 7, 9–10
McCaughey, Kenny, 7, 9–10
Mental illness, 46
Meritocratic society, 67–68
Merrick, Zannah, 44
MicroSort technology, 77
Mitochondrial DNA, 25
Morality, 61–63, 66, 75
Mundy, Liza, 81–91
Murdock, Alison, 36

N

Nachtigall, Robert, 85–90
National Bioethics Commission, 30
National Institutes of Health, 15, 35
Nazis, 61
New life for sale: Human eggs focus of booming $3B industry (Marcotty, Yee), 100
New York International Fringe Festival, 98–99
New York Times, 46, 98–99

Newcastle Centre for Life, 36
Newsweek, 93
Nicoll, Eleanor, 8
Northwestern University School of Medicine, 86
Nuremburg Laws, 61

O

Observer (newspaper), 105, 108, 110–112
Occupation, Safety and Health Administration, 31
Octuplets, 7
Ohio, 44
Oocyte preservation, 93
Ooplasm transfer, 25, 34, 49–50
Organ sales, 104
Our Possible Future (Fukuyama), 33
Ovarian hyperstimulation syndrome (OHSS), 100, 109
Ovarian stimulation, 99–103, 106–109

P

Parenthood
    biology as important, 40–41
    children's rights and, 40–41
    delay, 92–95
    hubris of parents, 64–65
    hyperparenting, 65–66
    legal questions of parenthood, 48–49
    meaning, 39, 40–42
    right to parent, 40
    surrogate gestation, 49
    William May's description, 22
    See also Donor-conceived children

Parkinson's disease, 90
Pence, Gregory, 12–15
Pennsylvania, 45
Perdue, 17
Petra Health Clinic, 110, 111
Physical appearance, 57–58
Planned Parenthood, 61
Poland, 112
Politiken: Technologie-Beratung, 24
Poultry industry, 16–17, 22
Poverty, 46
Pre-embryos, 83
Preimplantation genetic diagnosis (PGD)
    application, 26–27
    congenital disease prevention and, 37, 55, 57–58
    government regulation and, 30, 34–35, 37
    sex selection and, 27, 70
President's Council on Bioethics, 57
Pro-life advocates, 30
Progesterone, 103
Psychological issues, 8, 52–53

R

Racism, 77
Rae, Scott B., 7
Rand Consulting Group, 82
Reason (magazine), 33
Red blood cell function, 59
Regulation. *See* Government regulation
Reproductive control
    ART and, 21
    cloning and, 19–20
    contraception, 36–37, 85

customized children and, 63
life's beginnings and, 84–85
Reproductive Genetics Institute in
Chicago, 110
Reproductive-medicine specialists,
9
Reproductive technology
applications, 29–30
baby's health risks, 8
birth defects and, 8
controversy over, 29–30
disease inheritance and, 21
government regulation, 9, 26–
27, 48
informed consent and, 43
insurance coverage, 12, 13
jargon, 18
mother's risks, 7–8
poultry industry compared
with, 16–17
premature births and, 8
sex-selection technology, 20
success rates for, 13
uniformity and, 17
See also Risk; specific technologies
Reproductive tourism, 78
Research
egg donation aftereffects, 96,
97, 102–103
embryos and, 81–82
government regulation, 15
human embryos and, 14–15
sex selection and, 71–73
stem cells and, 30, 36, 83–84,
90, 100
Rifkin, Jeremy, 12
Risk
baby's health risks, 8
children of divorced parents
and, 46

children of single mothers
and, 46
donation of eggs and, 96–104
genetic enhancement and, 58
government regulation and,
28
infant mortality, 46
mother's health risks, 7–8
research and, 25
Roe v. Wade, 37, 83
Roosevelt, Theodore, 61
Rose, Joanna, 44
Rosenfeld, David L, 9
Russia, 110, 111

S

Safety issues. See Risk
Salisbury University, 16
Saltz, Gail, 8
San Francisco Film Festival, 98
Sanger, Margaret, 61
Science News, 14
Seizures, 8
Sen, Amartya, 76
Septuplets, 7
Sex-linked genetic disorders, 77
Sex selection
advertising and, 78
devaluation of women and, 70
discrimination against females
and, 69–70, 72
ethics, 69–80
ethnic groups and, 69, 71, 73,
78–79
family balancing and, 70–72,
74, 78
female child as preference,
71–72
government regulation and,
30, 35, 37, 58

in vitro fertilization (IVF)
and, 70, 77
male child as preference, 69–
72, 74, 76, 77, 79
marriage security and, 79
pre-natal testing and, 77
preimplantation genetic diagnosis (PGD) and, 70, 77
reproductive control and, 20,
26, 27
research on, 71–73
sperm sorting and, 70, 77
techniques for, 77–78
Sexism, 69, 70, 72, 76, 77
Shekar, Preeti, 76–80
Sickle cell anemia, 57
Smith, Helena, 105–112
Snyderman, Nancy, 8
Society for Assisted Reproductive
Technology, 82
Socioeconomic class, 62, 95
Soika, Karen, 92–93, 95
Solidarity, 66
Somatic cell nuclear transfer, 30
Somatic gene modification, 56–57
Sperm
intracytoplasmic sperm injection (ICSI), 18
sex selection and, 70
sperm donation/banks, 16, 20,
42–44, 48–49, 107
sperm sorting, 34, 70
stem cell creation of sperm,
26, 34, 50
trade in human sperm, 26, 35
See also Donor-conceived chil-
dren
St. Augustine, 23
Stanford Center for Biomedical
Ethics, 9

Stem cells
egg creation and, 26, 34, 50
research, 30, 36, 83–84, 90,
100
sperm creation and, 26, 34, 50
Sterilization, 33, 36, 61
Suicide, 46
Suleman, Nadya, 7–10
Surrogate gestation, 49
Sweden, 10
Switzerland, 24

T

Texas, 26, 34, 44
Thanos, Vasillis, 110–111
Time (magazine), 18
Tissue matching, 26
Today (TV program), 99
Transgenetic humans, 57
Tribe, Laurence, 52–53
Triplet Connection, 82
Triplets, 8, 81–82
Tucker, Patrick, 55–59

U

Ukraine, 105–106, 108, 110, 111
UNICEF, 79
Uniformity, 17
United Kingdom
donor-conceived children and,
44
government regulation of reproduction, 58, 71, 80, 97
sex selection and, 58, 71, 80
trade in human eggs and, 103,
104, 110
United Nations, 70, 72, 75
United Nations Convention on the
Rights of the Child, 40

Universal health-care system, 10
University of Alabama School of
    Medicine, 12
University of California at Irvine,
    14
University of California at San
    Francisco, 85
U.S. Congress
    Comstock Law, 36
    egg donor registry and, 97
    regulation of reproduction
        technology and, 14, 28–30
U.S. Department of Energy, 31
U.S. House of Representatives, 84
U.S. Post Office, 36
U.S. Supreme Court, 33, 36
USA Today (newspaper), 92
Uterine cancer, 103

V

Vaccines, 55, 57
Vanderkam, Laura, 92–95
Vatican, 13
Virginia, 14
Virginia, Loving v., 37

W

Wade, Roe v., 37, 83
Werlin, Lawrence, 8
Westchester Institute for Ethics
    and the Human Person, 57
Women, 69–70, 75

Y

Yale University School of Medi-
    cine, 69